Victory's Journey

MOVING ON
LEADER'S MANUAL

Laverne Weber Ministries

LAVERNE WEBER
WITH HEIDI GREGORY

VICTORY'S JOURNEY'S MOVING ON LEADER'S MANUAL

Copyright © 2010 by Laverne Weber and Heidi Gregory

"All rights reserved. No portion of this book may be reproduced, stored in a retrieval system, or transmitted in any form or by any means—electronic, mechanical, photocopy, recording, scanning, or other—except for brief quotations in reviews or articles, without the prior written permission of the author, with the exception of pages designated as reproducible for ministry purposes:

Bible References:

Unless otherwise specified, all Scripture quotations in this book are taken from THE HOLY BIBLE, NEW INTERNATIONAL VERSION®, NIV® Copyright © 1973, 1978, 1984, 2011 by Biblica, Inc.® Used by permission. All rights reserved worldwide.

Scripture quotations marked (ESV) are from ESV® Bible (The Holy Bible, English Standard Version®), copyright © 2001 by Crossway, a publishing ministry of Good News Publishers. Used by permission. All rights reserved.

Scripture quotations marked (AMP) are taken from the Amplified® Bible (AMP), Copyright © 2015 by The Lockman Foundation. Used by permission.

Scripture quotations marked (NASB) are taken from the New American Standard Bible® (NASB), Copyright © 1960, 1962, 1963, 1968, 1971, 1972, 1973, 1975, 1977, 1995 by The Lockman Foundation Used by permission.

Scripture quotations marked (NLT) are taken from the Holy Bible, New Living Translation, copyright © 1996, 2004, 2007 by Tyndale House Foundation. Used by permission of Tyndale House Publishers, Inc., Carol Stream, Illinois 60188. All rights reserved.

Scripture quotations marked (AMPC) are taken from the Amplified® Bible (AMPC), Copyright © 1954, 1958, 1962, 1964, 1965, 1987 by The Lockman Foundation. Used by permission.

NOTE: While the stories in this book are based on true events the details and names have been changed to protect the anonymity of those involved.

Design: 4One Ministries

Subject Headings: 1. Counseling   2. Discipleship   3. Personal Growth

ISBN: 978-0-9991966-2-5

Printed in the United States of America. All rights reserved.

What People Are Saying About Victory's Journey's Moving On:

"We each have a story. When our story is connected to God's story, He can bring healing and wholeness to our brokenness. In *Victory's Journey*, Laverne Weber offers hope and practical help to those who have been hurt through the tragedy of abuse. I highly recommend this manual as a resource for all of us."

-**Bryan Koch**, *PennDel District Assemblies of God Assistant Superintendent, Senior Pastor at GT Church West Lawn, Reading, PA, founder of Brian Koch Ministries, Author, and Speaker*

"*Victory's Journey* Ministries is an excellent training course designed to help men and women deal with the emotional pain of their past. This course designed by Rev. Weber is well organized and easy to follow. While utilizing psychological principles, the material remains biblically sound.

The *Victory's Journey* Manual is a complete tool and is presented in a concise and clear manner. It offers instruction for group facilitators as well as providing a basic format for each of the group meetings. Having served as a pastor and a mental health therapist, I strongly recommend this program. "

-**Dr. David Scolforo**, *Professor: University of Valley Forge*

"People come into our churches just as they are—with wounds that have held them back from experiencing the joy of their salvation and inhibited in their ability to love and serve the Lord and others. *Victory's Journey* addresses this serious issue by providing a process for healing that we believe is critical to Christian discipleship.

We have seen men and women being released from encumbrances and freed to fulfill God's purpose for their lives."

- **Chaplain John Puleo**, *MA, Board Certified Professional Counselor*
- **Ruth Puleo**, *Women of Purpose Director, PennDel District Assemblies of God*

"We've been using *Victory's Journey* small groups for ten years and many lives have been impacted and changed by the truth of God's word and the healing process as presented in Laverne Weber's curriculum.

I was immensely relieved in 2007 when Laverne shared her curriculum with us for helping women overcome the devastatingly shameful consequences of sexual, physical and emotional abuse. I had traveled my own healing journey with the Holy Spirit and God's Word so I found it exciting to see much of the same process revealed in her original curriculum, *Journey to Joy.*

The ladies found this small group to be a safe place to process their pain, interact about what they were learning and receive help in exchanging the ashes of rejection and abuse for the beauty of a new identity in Christ.

I highly recommend *Victory's Journey* small groups."

-**Angela M. Coon**, *Author, Speaker, Blog: Hand Me Downs www.angelamcoon.com*

"For the past eight years, ***Victory's Journey*** has been an integral component of our ministry at Newport Assembly of God Church. The combination of Biblical truth and small group support is central to the study. We have seen dozens of women and men move from painful pasts to freedom in Christ.

But ***Victory's Journey*** doesn't stop there. The program also equips for the future so participants do not repeat the patterns that cause so much frustration in their lives.

I can't tell you the number of times I have heard women talking to other women and saying, "***Victory's Journey*** taught me...."

I feel honored to recommend this program to anyone searching for more of Christ in their life."

Rev. Kristen Hill, *Newport Assembly of God Women's Pastor*

"***Victory's Journey*** was instrumental in my healing. The love and acceptance found in this small group ministry helped me look at my past and release the pain, shame and guilt that was defining who I was. Today I am free to move into all God has for me knowing that I am His and He is mine."

-**Pamela Wisniewski**, *Small Group Leader*

DEDICATION

To all the men and women of courage who have completed this program
and found their victory in Jesus!

ACKNOWLEDGEMENTS

I would like to thank all those who have worked so hard from the very first to help me make this manual and this ministry a reality. There are many who have contributed with their thoughts and encouragement and with editing, typing and printing the material. I would especially like to thank Heidi Gregory, Pam Wisniewski, Gretchen Duff, Tina Kester, John Puleo, and my husband, Pat.

Thank you to Jamie Holden and Adessa Holden for helping me publish this curriculum, making it available for others to use and obtain victory in their lives.

Most of all, I'd like to thank my precious Heavenly Father who birthed a seed in my heart and then fanned it into a flame. May this ministry always bring glory to His name!

. . . being confident of this, that he who began a good work in you will carry it on to completion until the day of Christ Jesus. - Philippians 1:6

Victory's Journey Ministries

Dear Pastors and Future Leaders,

There are many wounded people in the body of Christ. They may be so weighed down with pain that they cannot be all God desires them to be. God wants to minister to them and He calls us to carry His love and healing. As you step out in Victory's Journey Ministries, it is my prayer that God will bless you and make you a blessing.

I did not realize how great the need was for such a ministry until the summer of 1993 when I was asked if I would start a support group for women who'd been abused and were still dealing with the effects of that trauma. I answered that I would prayerfully consider it.

As I prayed, God filled me with a great compassion and birthed a vision within my heart. That fall we started our first group with four ladies. Other groups followed. Later the ministry expanded to include groups for men and teens. It has been awesome to watch the Lord heal damaged emotions in many areas. Those who were too shame-filled to raise their hands in praise are now reaching out to pray with others. Men and women who felt "if anyone in church knew my past they wouldn't want to talk to me" now share their story and lead groups.

Our church has been blessed by the after-waves as group members realize God really loves them. Those involved develop strong bonds with one another, and then reach out to others. Superficial greetings have been replaced by expressions of deep concern. Love and unity flow to others who are hurting. Facing issues and dealing with them according to Biblical guidelines helps those involved become all God intends for them.

This ministry has learned a lot as we have developed our own groups and we would like an opportunity to share that information with you. God's will for the hurting is that they might experience His love, and be able to pass it on to others. Through the acceptance, love, and support they receive in these small groups this becomes more than a vision statement; it becomes reality!

May God bless you as you prepare to step forward in this arena of ministry!

Sincerely,

Laverne Weber

Rev. Laverne Weber, Director

CONTENTS

Section One: Overview

    Our Story 11

    Purpose, Key Verse, Motto 12

    Victory's Journey Progression 13

Section Two: Leadership

    Leaders & Co-Leaders 17

    Leading from the Heart 18

    Handling Special Situations 23

    Legal Responsibilities 28

Section Three: Preparation for Group Ministry

    Preparation for Group Ministry 31

    Promotion 33

    The Interview 34

    Group Guidelines for Members 37

    Teen VJ Guidelines 40

    Group Dynamics 43

    Closure 49

Section Four: Guidelines

    Meeting Format 51

Section Five: Lesson Plans

    Week One: What are Feelings? 55

    Week Two: What is Pain? 65

    Week Three: Who is God? – Part 1 71

    Week Four: Who is God? - Part 2 75

    Week Five: The Power of God's Word 81

    Week Six: Love and Approval 83

Week Seven: Loss and Grief	85
Week Eight: What Does Your Past Look Like?	89
Week Nine: Secrets To Defeating Sin	95
Week Ten: Our Confidence	103
Week Eleven: Who Am I?	107
Week Twelve: Truth or Lies?	111
Week Thirteen: Freedom from Anger	115
Week Fourteen: Caring for One Another	119
Week Fifteen: Pain and Shame	121
Week Sixteen: Rebuilding the Ruins	125
Week Seventeen: Dealing with Negative Words	129
Week Eighteen: Healthy Confrontation	131
Week Nineteen: Forgiveness	133
Week Twenty: Healthy Relationships	137
Week Twenty-one: Change	141
Week Twenty-two: Boundaries	143
Week Twenty-three: Complete Surrender	147
Week Twenty-four: Victory	151

Section Six: Ministry Helps

Additional Topics for Journaling and Sharing	155
References & Recommended Reading	156
Contracts	157
Personal History	160
Personal Evaluation	162
Letters	164

SECTION 1:
OVERVIEW

Our Story

Everyone has a story!

Our story began when one lady who had a story encountered other ladies with similar stories. She realized she wasn't alone with a pain-filled past and she asked for help. She asked if there could be a small group that could minister to women with abuse in their past. Oh, she wasn't going to attend herself, just help some other ladies get started. Another lady agreed to be the hostess. This lady was just going to help, too. Another just came to be with a friend.

But...God!

When God gets involved things really get exciting. That is just what happened. Somehow the lady who started it all, who wasn't even going to come herself, ended up in that first group. She didn't expect too much. After all, she didn't get very emotional...she didn't even cry.

But...God!

The leader mentioned one particular word and something inside her broken heart responded. The tears started to flow. The healing began... and continued...and passed on to others, men and women and teens.

    And the story continues...

        Because...

            Now it is your story, too!

Our Purpose, Key Verse & Motto

"Victory's Journey" is a ministry dedicated to helping emotionally and spiritually wounded people find healing through small sharing groups. We believe that by establishing an atmosphere of acceptance and confidentiality, they will feel free to take a look at their pain and deal with it according to Scriptural principles.

By sharing, praying, and learning to apply God's Word together, those in the group grow into being the people God intended. As they support one another, and hold each other accountable, they experience God's unconditional love.

The leaders in these groups are not professional counselors, but they are caring and supportive with a desire to reach out and give a helping hand. Training seminars are also available. (There may be times when we encourage a group member to seek one-on-one counseling from a professional counselor.)

Our Purpose

Jesus Christ offers abundant life, and it is God's desire to see His sons and daughters enjoy the life He gives. He wants us to be all we can be in Him. His Word has so many promises for those who follow His ways. We suggest you encourage the members to write these verses on cards and carry them with them until they become a part of their thought patterns.

> *"You have made known to me the paths of life; you will fill me with joy in your presence." - Acts 2:28*

> *"For I know the plans I have for you," declares the Lord, "plans to prosper you and not to harm you, plans to give you hope and a future." - Jeremiah 29:11*

Key Verse

> *"Being confident of this, that he who began a good work in you will carry it on to completion until the day of Christ Jesus." - Philippians 1:6*

Motto: Look and Live

God wants us to face our pain, to look at it. It is a part of our history and ignoring it will only produce more pain. When we identify the thing that holds us back we can really give it to Jesus. Letting go and trusting our loving God allows us to live the abundant life Jesus promised to all His followers in John 10:10.

Section 1: Overview

Victory Journey's Progression
"Victim"

1. Painful event

2. Warped view of God, self, and others

3. Denial

    A. Stuff feelings, turn off emotionally

    B. Block memories

    C. Separating from experiences - "This didn't happen to me".

    D. Masks

    E. Minimizing

    F. Physical symptoms

4. Realization of a problem with possible symptoms such as fear, guilt, nightmares, panic attacks, anger, promiscuity, shame, addictions

5. Anger/hate

    A. Towards others (may not be abuser)

    B. Towards self (depression, mutilation, suicidal thoughts)

    C. Towards God ("Why did He let this happen to me?")

6. Reaching out for help through counseling and/or group (Despite fears, putting oneself in group with intention of developing close relationships and sharing pain.)

7. Beginning to share: facts, then fears, anger, needs, and shame

    A. Acceptance by group (Acceptance enhanced by being prayed with)

    B. Sense of safety

    C. Journaling

    D. Sharing within group (James 5:16 and Ps 32:3)

    E. Prayer (at times spiritual warfare) and thankfulness

    F. Tears

    G. Fasting

Moving On

    H. God's Word

    I. Accountability

8. Acknowledgement of pain, with validation of that pain by others

    A. Increased vulnerability as walls begin to come down

    B. Grief process

    C. Awareness of personal reactions and responses

        1. Avoiding "martyr syndrome", attention-seeking, blaming

        2. Receiving love/approval

    D. Learning to develop positive relationships

9. Putting responsibility where it belongs

    A. Sharing in group

    B. Letter writing

    C. Ability to reject false guilt

    D. Taking responsibility for own (present) actions

    E. Renouncing past life-styles, behaviors, and addictions that prevent the growth of Christlike virtues

10. Sharing with spouse or a close friend (as led by the Holy Spirit)

11. Confrontation (when led by the Holy Spirit)

    A. Moving from vulnerability into a whole new life style

    B. May need balancing and boundaries

12. Choosing to release the past to God

13. Trading obsessive thoughts for thoughts from God's perspective

    A. Praying and praising God for who He is

    B. Journaling or drawing

    C. Reading and meditating (ex. Ps 91 and Ps 23)

    D. Calling a brother or sister (or your leader)

14. Forgiveness by choice

   A. Of self

   B. Of God

   C. Of abuser(s)

15. Peace, remembrance without pain or shame

16. Ability to reach out to others, enhanced ministry

17. Receiving a white stone, a symbol of winning, much like the key to the city

"Victor"

Note: As the group members deal with individual pains some recycling may be seen.

SECTION 2:
LEADERSHIP

Requirements For Leaders

1. Be born again through a personal acceptance of Jesus Christ as Lord and Savior.

2. Be filled with the Holy Spirit, seeking His power in ministry.

3. Be living a life of obedience to God's Word.

4. Be called by the Holy Spirit to this ministry.

5. Be united with your co-leader, standing together. Information is shared. Let your group know that if one knows you will both know.

6. Be in agreement with your spouse regarding this involvement.

7. Be approved by the local pastor and the leadership of the ministry. Stay loyal and accountable to those God has placed over you (Hebrews 13:17).

8. Pray for the other leader and your group members.

9. Keep a servant heart.

Additional Requirements for Co-Leaders

1. Write down any extra group or individual assignments. Ask for them at the next meeting.

2. Notify the group members of changes or special gatherings.

3. Be "there" when someone needs extra support.

4. Be prepared to lead the group if the leader is not able to make the meeting.

5. Feel free to make suggestions. You are there to add insights and to help recognize a potential problem before it gets worse. Sometimes the leader does not notice things you may see. You are a team. If God gives you something, share it. Encourage the leader. Be open to suggestions. You are working together, and as you do, you will both grow.

Note: The leaders may choose to share the teaching time

Leading from the Heart
Leadership Helps

Because Jesus loves you, you can love. Let that love and compassion flow from Christ, through you, and to those in your group. These are broken people who are hurting and hungry for love. God's love is the best love you can give them.

> *Love must be sincere. …Be devoted to one another in love. Honor one another above yourselves. Never be lacking in zeal, but keep your spiritual fervor, serving the Lord. Be joyful in hope, patient in affliction, faithful in prayer. Share with God's people who are in need. Practice hospitality. Bless those who persecute you; bless and do not curse. Rejoice with those who rejoice; mourn with those who mourn. Live in harmony with one another.*
> *- Romans 12:9-16*

You may have feelings of inadequacy. Everyone has them. Praise the Lord that you do, for these feelings keep us humble and dependent on the Holy Spirit's help. When you are open about your own struggles, such as feelings of inadequacy, those in your group will feel closer to you as their leader. On the other hand, if you focus on these you will undermine your effectiveness.

Remember, God is your Source.

Be Positive

At first, most of them just want to hear there is hope. Set an atmosphere of acceptance, love and trust. Remember, many of these people need to feel safe and accepted just as they are. They will watch you to see if you really will accept them and love them, even when they are expressing very strong feelings, such as hate.

If they seem to be "attacking" you it is probably because they feel you are "safe", that you are someone who will accept them anyway. If you know you have not failed them, do not take it personally, but establish some boundaries. If you are in the wrong, do what you need to do to make it right as soon as possible with a humble spirit.

Be an Encourager

Many of those in this ministry have been emotionally abused. They need liberal gifts of praise when they are moving in the right direction. As you demonstrate acceptance and respect for each person, others in the group will do the same. The person sharing will feel the support.

Those in your group may begin to see you as a parent or older sibling. They may even become overly dependent on you. If you are exhausted you cannot really minister. Setting limits with your time helps them in the long run. (Ask them to do the steps in "Victory's

Journey Progression, Number 13. Trading in obsessive thoughts for thoughts from God's perspective" on page 14 of their workbook before calling you.)

Be Able to Release

As the members grow they will become less dependent on the leaders. As they minister to one another they may not seem to need you as much. Be prepared to "let go". This is a sign you are doing your job well!

Listen From the Heart

Look at the person who is talking. Be aware of your body language and what you are communicating. Be alert to the words you are hearing, the tones in which they are spoken, and the body language that accompanies them. Ask questions to verify or to help focus on a particular point. Direct them to what their reaction might be with questions like, "How does that make you feel?"

One person may need to share, another may withdraw, and another may panic or become angry. Be sensitive to where each person is emotionally. While encouraging openness, avoid the use of coercion by others or yourself. Allow everyone an opportunity to be involved, while understanding that some may take time to feel comfortable.

Appropriate laughter is good medicine (Proverbs 17:22), especially when it is spontaneous. Just be alert to each person's response and be careful that laughter never becomes a put down.

Cards, notes, texts and phone calls play a key role in showing you care. If someone is dealing with a tough issue, be sure they know you are there for them. Pray for each member of your group. According to 2 Corinthians 1:3-4, God comforts us and helps us to comfort others.

Keep the progression of *"Victory's Journey"* in mind. Remind the group members of these goals often and of their commitment to change.

Encourage them to develop friendships but be alert to sub-groups. It is a good idea for them to share things in the group which have been shared one-on-one.

Testimonies

You may feel a need to share your testimony, or be asked to do so in another group. Please keep these principles in mind when doing so:

    A. Be real, honest, and open but do not share areas that are open hurts for you. (These should be shared with leaders who can support you.) Your purpose is to give hope.

    B. Have a basic outline. It will help you know where you are going...and when you are done.

C. Tell your story, using some specific examples. Too many examples can be depressing or make you testimony drag.

D. Spend more time on what God and group have done for you than on the negatives. Use Scriptures.

E. Look at them while you talk. Remember they are hurting, too. Your story may trigger some painful memories or feelings.

F. If it is not your group, look to the leader for direction before going to someone.

G. Be sensitive to the Holy Spirit.

Compassionate Confrontation

People come into *"Victory's Journey"* from a variety of different backgrounds. Acceptance is a key part of the effectiveness of the support group, but certain behavior issues may need to be addressed. The leader needs to communicate an acceptance of the person without condoning the behavior. His/her example may be enough. If not, give a gentle word of exhortation using Scriptural guidelines. This needs always to be done in humility and love with an understanding that growth takes time.

It is vital that the leaders stay on top of anything that might make someone uncomfortable and step in before any damage is done. This can be done by redirecting a comment or question back to the person who spoke it. You might respond with, "You seem to have a strong feeling about this. How does this situation make you feel?" If it is hurtful you can ask how they think the person addressed might feel about the way it was said. Ask, "What can our group learn from this?"

Most of us would like to avoid confrontation. However, real love is compassionately confrontational. As leaders, your purpose is to help each person grow and mature spiritually. That involves accountability before God.

Don't feel guilty when you need to challenge someone. You cannot make choices for others but your motive is to help them mature in Christ. Don't put off confrontation until you are frustrated, but deal with each situation as you are aware of it, in love.

In dealing with conflicts between two people, follow the pattern Jesus gave us in Matthew 18, verses 4 and 15-17:

> *Therefore, whoever takes the lowly position of this child is the greatest in the kingdom of heaven…If your brother or sister sins, go and point out their fault, just between the two of you. If they listen to you, you have won them over. But if they will not listen, take one or two others along, so that 'every matter may be established by the testimony of two or three witnesses.' If they still refuse to listen, tell it to the church; and if they refuse to listen even to the church, treat them as you would a pagan or a tax collector.*

Section 2: Leadership

In a situation within this ministry, going to the "church" would mean going to the local leadership of the ministry first, and then to the pastor. Inform the director of the situation so he/she is prepared if the person you are confronting calls. The director may be able to give you some suggestions, and will certainly be able to support you in prayer. It is also wise to document all that is said during any confrontation. So that nothing can be twisted later, both leaders need to be present. (If the person does not receive you, follow the pattern of Matthew 18:15-18. I Corinthians 5 gives a pattern for extreme situations, but this would come under the role of the director and board.)

Pray first that you are filled with God's love for the person you will confront. Pray that you know the direction the Lord would have you take in the issue involved. Pray for the person to be prepared to receive what you have to share. And pray with the person for God to continue to work out His will in his/her life. Prayer makes a difference!

And, remember, you are not responsible for the choices someone else makes. You are only responsible to do what God has asked you to do in warning them. Sometimes the hardest part is letting go and letting God do the rest.

You cannot help someone who does not want to change!

Memories

Avoid "feeding" or suggesting ideas that may lead to false memories. Memories should be treated as welcome guests, but not hunted down. Real memories will come in God's way at God's time. If memories come, make attempts to validate them. A validated memory protects the person from Satan's lies.

Personal Life

Being a leader can be hard work, and there are times when you will feel exhausted physically, emotionally, and spiritually. If you are totally worn out your ability to minister will be effected. Know your limits. Those in your family and your co-leader can help you realize when you need to back off and get some rest. One minister said, "There are times when the most spiritual thing we can do is get eight hours of sleep".

Boundaries are healthy. Just knowing you are praying for them will help your group members make it.

Maintain your own spiritual walk. (A good study is to examine the emotional and spiritual lives of key Bible leaders.) Seek counsel for your own needs. Have times of refreshment and just being in the Lord's presence. Enjoy your family.

Keep yourself in line with God's Word. Be careful that you do not condone sin, or any anti-Scriptural stance, because of being fearful. Jesus was compassionate but direct. If you are unsure of the position you should take, talk to those in leadership.

Moving On

Be alert to any early signs of discord between you and the other leader. Deal with issues promptly in love, each considering the other better than themselves (Philippians 2:3). Remember, your people may try to put one of you against another, just as children do with parents. Also, one in your group may connect more with one leader while another may feel closer to the other. This does not make any one better; it usually has to do with past experiences. If you can have some special prayer times together as leaders it will make you more of a team.

Be accountable to those God has placed in authority over you in ministry. Be supportive and encouraging to them. Pray for them.

Accept responsibility, influence by your life, and guide according to Scriptural principles. <u>Do not attempt to force an issue or a memory</u>. Just remember, the Holy Spirit is always there to guide you.

Be aware of your legal/moral responsibilities, such as reporting abuse. It is best to tell the person involved first what you intend to do.

One of the hardest parts of being a group leader is that you do not come totally equipped. There is no way to be completely prepared for each situation that will arise in each group, and there is no way to be experienced until you have experienced some of the tough times. The beautiful thing about doing this as a ministry is that the Holy Spirit does not send us out alone but He equips us!

> *But you will receive power when the Holy Spirit comes on you; and you will be my witnesses in Jerusalem, and in all Judea and Samaria, and to the ends of the earth. - Acts 1:8*

As you go in the name of Jesus, and as you are sensitive to the Holy Spirit, you will also be led by the Holy Spirit. And, if you are not sure how to deal with a situation, you can tell your group members you will discuss it the next week, after prayer, and talking it over with the ministry director.

Rely much on the Holy Spirit. Use your guidelines and helps, but be flexible if you know it is the Lord. Spend time waiting in God's presence before your meeting. The Holy Spirit and experience will help you.

Expect to see great results as God works to accomplish His purpose. God called and equipped you to minister to those He has given you. No one else would be quite like you in your approach so do not compare yourself to others, and do not put yourself down. You are God's gift to your little flock. It is a holy calling.

Section 2: Leadership

Handling Special Situations

1. Substance Use Disorder

Definition – "characterized by one or more of the following features: (1) a pattern of pathological use that involves frequent intoxication, a need for daily use, and an inability to control use – in a sense, psychological dependence; (2) a significant impairment of social or occupational functioning attributed to the drug use; and (3) physical dependence that involves serious withdrawal problems."

Suggestions for Handling – refer him/her to rehab counseling (such as Teen Challenge), confront, pray, provide safe travel home. Ask questions, such as: When was the last time you drank or used drugs? How often and how much at a time? Are others upset about your use of this substance?

2. Self-mutilation

Definition – "Injury, or attempted injury to a person's body, which is self-inflicted, purposefully or absentmindedly."

Remember that socially acceptable behavior is different for men and women. Women may be cutting, while men may punch walls. They may not see this as self-mutilation, but the result is pain inflicted on self.

Suggestions for Handling – Contract for safety, preoccupy hands, determine root cause (e.g. self-punishment, self-stimulation, release, to feel pain).

3. Panic Attacks

Definition – "a recurrent anxiety disorder marked by the sudden onset of intense apprehension or terror." Symptoms may include the following: feelings of impending doom, hyperventilation, chest pains, sweating or chills, flushing, dizziness, and agitation or a feeling of helplessness. A panic attack usually lasts 5 to 20 minutes.

Suggestions for Handling – Relax, breathe deeply (paper bag breathing), physical activity such as walking, gardening, knitting or painting. (Leader needs to remain calm and stay with the person.) Give some sugar in case sugar level is low. Encourage informing medical provider.

If you are unsure of what is happening call 911!

4. Suicidal Potential

Definition – The probability that a person will try to kill themselves.

The potential is determined by the following factors:

Moving On

1. Thoughts about death or killing oneself – This is a time when hope is needed.
2. A plan of how he/she would kill himself/herself – Ask questions. Refer.
3. The physical means of completing the plan - This is serious.
4. Intent to carry out the plan - Immediate help is needed. Stay with them until they are safe.

Suggestions for Handling –

DO:

- Be direct, but calm and caring. Be a good listener.
- Ask if the person is thinking of hurting themselves.
- Assess the seriousness by determining if the person has a developed plan and whom else they have talked with about this.
- Assist the person in getting professional help and maintaining safety. This may involve calling a crisis hot-line or 911.

DO NOT:

- Ignore the warning signs or give false assurance that "everything will be okay".
- Act scared or repulsed or disappointed.
- Refuse to talk about it if you are approached.
- Abandon the individual even if you feel the crisis is over, or they are receiving professional help. They still need a friend!

5. Child or Elder Abuse

Definition – "the physical or mental injury, sexual abuse, negligent treatment, or maltreatment of a child under the age of 18 by a person who is responsible for the child's welfare under circumstances which indicate that the child's health or welfare is harmed or threatened thereby". (Public Law 93-237). Elder abuse would apply to an older person who is not capable of caring for themselves.

There are four types: Physical abuse, sexual abuse, physical neglect and emotional abuse. Ongoing child abuse must be reported to Child Services. The national hot line number is 1-800-4-A-CHILD.

6. Violent Behavior

Definition – aggressive physical outbursts of hurtful energy, usually against another person. It might include hitting, kicking, spitting, intimidating actions, or even the use of weapons.

In the abuse cycle the abuser may be violent and then very remorseful, promising never to do it again. However, after the guilt fades, he/she will begin to verbally batter the victim. As the tension escalates so will the level of violence.

Suggestions for Handling – Separate the person. Do not try to hold them down. Keep a safe distance. Speak calmly, listen/hear them out. When one of the leaders is targeted he/she should stay with the group and the other leader should talk to the person. Do not go where the group cannot see and hear what is going on. If the situation escalates beyond your feeling capable to handle it, call 911.

7. Body Memories

Definition – memories that are related to sights, sounds, smells, or mind pictures.

Suggestions for Handling – The sensation should be treated as a memory. Suggest replacing it with a Bible verse. They can use a "remote control" to turn down the intensity or change the channel, or turn it off. Encourage them to journal.

8. Regression

Definition - going back in time mentally and reliving experiences or behavior.

Suggestions for Handling – Give support and bring Jesus into the scenario (i.e. "Open your eyes and look at those around you. We love you. Jesus is here. He loves you and wants to help keep you safe"). DO NOT try to make regression happen!

9. Demonic Manifestation

Definition – an overt expression of Satanic activity.

    Oppression – "on" – forces coming against godly behavior or actions

    Possession – "in" – demon(s) entering a person, controlling thoughts and behavior

Note: This is a very rarely encountered issue; however, it is included to help you as the leader be better prepared for any situation you may face. Satanic cults and activity are more prevalent in geographic regions where the area has a history of spiritual darkness and/or witchcraft.

<u>Be very careful of labeling someone demon-possessed</u>. The Bible teaches us that the Holy Spirit and demons cannot dwell together. However, if someone backslides they open their heart and mind to the enemy, especially if they have a history of devil activity.

Suggestions for Handling –

1. Watch, keep your eyes open

- Body signals – may convulse, become agitated or retreat, especially when people are praising Jesus. Voice changes are not that common.

- Eyes – may see changes in eyes, such as an evil presence.
- Spiritual resistance - The person won't want to be touched or prayed for. They will have difficulty saying, "Jesus is my Lord".

2. Pray

- <u>Be covered with the blood of Jesus and sure of your relationship in Him</u>. Pray in the Name of Jesus, the Christ. Command the demon(s) to leave.
- Have prayer back-up
- Be led of the Holy Spirit – 1 Corinthians 12:10 (Do they want to be free?)
- Pray in the Holy Spirit. You can anoint with oil.
- Be persistent. Stay with them until the situation is resolved. Do not restrain or prevent them from leaving. Do not carry on a conversation with any demons.
- Stay calm and confident in Christ Jesus. He has already defeated Satan.
- The person needs to renounce the demon and its effect on their life.
- They need to resolve any sin that has been allowed by confessing it and asking Jesus to forgive them.
- Remember this is a spiritual battle.

3. Follow-up

- Immediate and frequent follow-up and mentoring in the Word of God is necessary. The victims of satanic ritual abuse may have been told many lies.

There are three main truths that win over the enemy's lies. They are as follows:

1. Satan is real.
2. God is greater.
3. God's Truth sets us free from Satan's power.

The leader(s) may need an opportunity to vent and receive ministry.

10. Major Depression

Definition – decrease in joy and in the ability to find pleasure in life, lack of ability to concentrate, insomnia or excessive sleeping, unexplainable sadness and crying. It may be due to a chemical imbalance in the body.

Suggestions for Handling – Ask them if they are having a lot of dark or gloomy thoughts. Ask if they are having any thoughts of hurting themselves. If the person is considering suicide, help them find a reputable counselor or call the crisis hot-line. Stay with them until they are "safe".

If they are not suicidal, help them learn who they are in Christ. They may need help in dealing with difficult issues or in looking forward to life events. Pray for freedom for them to be the person God has created and give emotional support. (You may need to set some boundaries.) In severe depression medications are often needed to replace important chemicals.

Crisis Evaluation

Determine the seriousness of the situation. Be attentive to the person as they explain how they feel. Ask the person if they are willing to get help. <u>Ask the person to contract with you to follow guidelines for safety</u>. Do not attempt to handle any threatening situation alone. Refer to a reliable mental health professional.

Legal Responsibilities

Leaders in this ministry are not licensed counselors; they are simply Christians who care. As a ministry, our purpose is to promote spiritual healing through applying the principles of God's Word and prayer. By offering love and acceptance in a "safe" place, hurting people can look at their pain and find healing. It is our desire to help those in our groups to find new life, and then to reach out to others with that same comfort.

> *Praise be to the God and Father of our Lord Jesus Christ, the Father of compassion and the God of all comfort, who comforts us in all our troubles, so that we can comfort those in any trouble with the comfort we ourselves received from God. -2 Corinthians 1:3,4*

Despite the fact that we are not professional counselors, we have a responsibility not to cause anyone more pain, or bring any reproach upon the name of Jesus. Take notes of situations that you may need to remember.

From the initial interview we stress confidentiality, for without confidentiality there would not be the trust needed for group members to share personal and painful information. Trust is a gift.

Group members may share their own involvement, but they are not to share the identities of others in the group, including the leaders, unless that permission has been granted. They are also not to share specific information that might reveal anything about anyone else in the group. We do our part by reminding the members periodically. They are told that the director and the pastoral advisor will know the names of those in each group, and if their leader needs some guidance or prayer about a specific situation, he/she will seek counsel from them. Should someone break a confidence the leaders and the director will deal with it together. Usually, the person will be asked to leave "*Victory's Journey*".

Those in leadership are committed to keeping confidentiality unless there is a danger to the person involved or to another. Such dangers include the threat of suicide, murder, abuse, property damage, or the passing on of diseases. In this case the leader must do what he/she feels is best for all involved. Tell what you must report early on in the group so there are no surprises. Some states require that child and elder abuse be reported. In Pennsylvania, child abuse should be reported to ChildLine at 1-800-932-0313. A national number is 1-800-4-A-CHILD. Know your state laws regarding mandated reporting and where to report. All of us should report abuse because we care.

As a support ministry, we encourage anyone on medication to take that medication as prescribed by their doctor. While God heals both physically and emotionally, He sometimes uses doctors to help in this healing. Be aware of medications your people are taking so you can encourage them to keep up with their prescriptions.

Do not make promises you cannot keep. Remember, our purpose is to point the way. The healing happens as each member and God work together. Our role is one of continuous encouragement to keep on working towards the goal.

SECTION 3:
PREPARATION FOR GROUP MINISTRY

Why Do You Want to Start a Group?

Why would you choose a group ministry for your church? In the book of Acts, chapter 2, we read about the close fellowship and unity of the early church as they "*broke bread together in their homes*". In the last few years there has been an increased awareness of the value of these small groups, both in the church and in the field of counseling.

An obvious advantage is the small size of the group. While people might share some things during a Bible study at the church, most would not feel comfortable sharing very personal and painful information with that many people. Another advantage is the security of knowing that others in this group have similar pains and problems and, therefore, understand the importance of confidentiality. A sense of family develops resulting in a "being there" for each other. *"Carry each other's burdens, and in this way you will fulfill the law of Christ" (Galatians 6:2)* becomes a way of life. Participants who have had difficulty with relationships learn to be true friends. In the process, it is easier to develop a more loving and biblically sound relationship with God.

The group also involves commitment. We have noted that those who do not have a strong reason for being involved will not stick it out. Those who want to see changes in their lives will do the work that is asked, even when it is difficult. With the support of those who know and care, they will begin to practice new ways of living, exchanging the "old" for the "new". Making choices based on God's Word opens doors and allows freedom to experience Christ's abundant life. There is guidance and accountability as they step out in new areas, and this increases the security factor. The results are not immediate, but they are exciting. Many of those who began in group overwhelmed by their pain are able to grow to the point of reaching out to others.

Why would you choose a group ministry for your church? Because the positive effects of those who complete the program and then reach out have a ripple effect on the whole congregation. The church feels their love and concern, and the pastors have helpers in the work of the ministry.

Who Will Lead the Group?

As Paul instructed Timothy in 1 Timothy 4:12 in regard to his leadership, a leader should be one who can *"set an example for the believers in speech, in conduct, in love, in faith and in purity"*. Potential leaders should know beyond any doubt that they are called to this ministry. Once committed, it is so important that they realize this is a long term commitment that will be very demanding at times. To leave a group in midstream can cause feelings of rejection and abandonment for those in the group. Therefore, leaders should be reliable and trustworthy, having proven themselves in their Christian walk. They should also be loyal to the church and to the ministry of "*Victory's Journey*", so that they promote unity, and not division, in the body of Christ.

One of the first steps in starting a group is to schedule a meeting of the leadership and the pastor to review the goals and plans for having such a ministry. This promotes understanding and support, and gives unity of purpose. We also recommend that leaders be accountable to their pastor and to the leaders of their local "*Victory's Journey*" ministry. This is a protection against false doctrine and potentially harmful practice

What Is Your Plan?

Before announcing the proposed ministry, there are several questions to be resolved:

1. Where Will You Meet?

While groups can meet at the church, it would need to be at a time and in a place where they would not be disturbed. It is also important that the identity of those in the group be shielded, as most will want to keep their involvement private. Meeting in a quiet private home setting may promote a greater sense of security.

2. When Will You Meet?

To be effective, groups need to meet weekly. The time will depend on the schedules of the leaders and potential group members. Allow for two hours, but meetings may occasionally run longer. During holidays groups usually meet every other week.

3. How Long Will Your Group Last?

Generally 6 months, sometimes longer, especially if you incorporate the suggestions under "Additional Topics for Journaling and Sharing". While this sounds like a long time, we must remember that the participants in the group did not develop their need for such a ministry in a short time. God deals with pain one layer at a time. To rush the process may do more damage than good. It takes time to rebuild broken lives into healthy ones.

4. How Large Should a Group Be?

A group of three to five, plus two leaders, seems to work best. This allows for the fact that one or two may drop out after the first month or so. If the group is too large members seem to be inhibited in their initial sharing. The material may be used in individual ministry.

5. Can We Add to the Group After It Starts?

It is possible to add someone to the group without too much upheaval early in the process. It is also possible at times to bring someone in at a later date. However, this needs to be done with much prayer and the permission of everyone already in the group.

Section 3: Preparation For Group Ministry

Promotion

Suggestions for Announcing a "*Victory's Journey*" Ministry:

1. Inform the church board about the ministry. Ask them to covenant to pray for the ministry, the leaders, and those who will be involved, even though they will not know who they are.

2. Inform the church congregation about the ministry and why you have chosen to start such a ministry. Ask for prayer support.

3. Announce what month it will begin. Invite those who are interested to contact a pastor, a leader, or the office to leave their name and phone number.

   A sample announcement might read:

   "We believe God is leading us to minister to those in the body of Christ who are hurting because of things in their past that have caused pain and shame. Jesus offers us abundant life. His Word gives us principles for gaining victory over difficult areas.

   In (month) _____, we plan to begin a small group ministry called "*Victory's Journey*". If you are interested, or would just like some more information, please contact _____. (Names will be kept confidential.)"

4. Contact people personally that you feel may be interested. Limit to one time and then let them know they are welcome to contact you anytime about future groups. Your excitement will give some people the hope they need.

5. Get back to people that are interested promptly. Remember that it took a lot of courage to make a contact. They will be waiting anxiously to hear from you.

6. When you talk to someone who is interested explain how the ministry works and about the interview process. Set up a time to meet with them for the interview.

7. If the group does not start in the near future, keep in touch with those who are interested so they will not become discouraged.

The Interview

The interview is an opportunity to inform a prospective group member about "*Victory's Journey*", what it is, how it works, and what they might expect. The leaders can get an idea of how ready and willing the person is to work at their healing. It is the interview which helps the leaders sense if someone will benefit from this ministry, and if he/she will be a benefit to others in this group setting.

The group leaders may already know those interested in being involved in a "*Victory's Journey*" group. Even if this is so, it is important to hold the interview. It can be a time for getting better acquainted. It may also be a time for ministry. In fact, if someone is unsure of their stance in Christ, it may be an opportunity to lead them to the Lord.

It is important to remember that no commitments should be made prior to the interview. There is always the possibility that something would come up that would change the decision and it is much easier to say "no" if you haven't already said, or implied, "yes".

Interview Procedure

1. Determine when and where the interviews will take place, and who will be present. Usually both leaders and the director are present. If the director is not able to be there, he/she will work out some guidelines with the leaders. It is very important that both leaders are present as this is also a vital bonding time that establishes future relationships.

2. Plan what part each of the leaders will have in the interview. Both leaders should take part as one of the goals of the interview is to get acquainted. Have an understanding that both may add their thoughts, as long as they do not interrupt each other.

   Highlighting key words helps you to avoid missing important points.

3. Notify each prospective member of their interview time. It is best to schedule an hour per appointment. This is often the place where they will begin to open up as they sense love and acceptance. The ministry that follows takes time and should not be rushed.

4. Leaders should pray individually and meet early to pray for the direction of the Holy Spirit. God puts people together as He sees fit, and when He does, the results are beautiful. We need His guidance.

5. Be ready to begin on time. Those waiting their turn are already nervous.

6. Welcome the prospective group member with warmth and kindness.

7. Open the interview with a prayer for God's love and direction.

Section 3: Preparation For Group Ministry

8. Ask how the person heard about "*Victory's Journey*".

9. Explain the purpose of "Victory's Journey ". Talk about the key verse and motto (page 12). Remind them that God cares about His hurting children. Discuss the guidelines (pages 37), being sure to include honesty, openness, and confidentiality.

10. Give an idea of what one might expect in a meeting. The person being interviewed will want to know how often and where the meetings will be held, how long they last, and how large the group will be.

11. Talk about commitment, yours and theirs. Help each person understand that it is a difficult journey, and that they may actually feel worse for a while as they face the past. However, as they work with the Lord, they will see victories...and they will not be alone. If appropriate, share briefly your testimony. Give hope by telling of some of the changes others have experienced. (Maintain confidentiality! Just use words like freedom from fear, guilt, etc.)

12. Ask if they feel ready to face the issues that have held them back. Can they make this commitment? Are they willing to do the work involved in the healing process? Is their family supportive? Discuss the policy for absenteeism.

13. Explain that the first month is a time to see if they still feel this is what they should do, and a chance for us to get a sense of whether this is beneficial for them at this time. Group is not the answer for everyone and so there is no embarrassment in finding out it is not the best answer right now.

14. Ask if there are any questions.

15. What expectations do they have? Ask questions, but do not probe.

16. Remind him/her that the leaders are not trained counselors, and it may be helpful to also seek a reputable therapist. Ask if the person is receiving, or has received, counseling. Is he/she on any medications? Have they ever been diagnosed with a physical or mental health problem that might affect their involvement in the group? Reassure them that others with problems who are on medications have been helped by this ministry. We only ask for this information to help us minister to needs. It will not be used against them.

Have the person sign the "Victory's Journey Member Contract" (page 157) and fill out the "Confidential Personal History" form (pages 160-161). It is best that it be filled out and returned immediately.

17. Ask them to be in prayer, and let them know you will be praying. If they decide that this is not for them at this time, ask that they let you know. Set a time (no more than 48 hours) for letting the person know your decision to accept them into the group.

18. Close in a prayer that God will help us all to make the right decisions. He knows what will be best for each one in the long run, and we need His guidance.

19. Leaders should pray individually and then share their answers. If there is a question it may be necessary to talk to the person again, and you will want to spend more time in prayer. It may be helpful to talk to the pastor.

20. Contact him/her to give your answer. This does not need to be lengthy unless you have more questions or need to explain a negative decision.

Questions for Leaders to Ask Themselves After the Interview:

- Is there a sense of openness and need?

- Is there a willingness to do whatever work is needed to achieve change?

- Is the person receptive to suggestions? Is this person open to hearing godly principles? Will he/she be able to handle being challenged in love?

- Does the person seem stable enough at this point to deal with painful issues?

- Is he/she able to share some personal things, even though it may be only small bits of information?

- Is he/she so talkative that others may not feel they can share?

- Is he/she aggressive?

- Is there any sense of judgment towards others?

- Is there a reputation for keeping confidences?

- Is this someone known as one who keeps his/her word.

- What direction does the Holy Spirit seem to be leading?

Remember, if you feel someone is not ready at this time for "*Victory's Journey*", it may be that to place them in such a setting would do more harm to them and may cause difficulties for others in the group. Whether the answer is yes, or not right now, you are doing what you feel is best for them.

Section 3: Preparation For Group Ministry

Group Guidelines For Members

These guidelines will help the individual heal and the group be successful. Share them at the interview and several times in the first few months. They are as follows:

1. Be Honest

You will receive only as much from this group as you are willing to share of yourself. No one will insist that you tell any details that you do not wish to tell. However, as you verbalize your memories you will benefit. You will not be rushed, so take your time as you tell what is bothering you. Remember truth sets us free.

2. Be a Confidante

Because people in this group will be sharing secrets from their past, it is essential that these things be kept within the group. It is also important that the names of those in the group be kept confidential. DO NOT even discuss these things with your spouse or closest friend (who you know will never tell). Sometimes little things might be allowed to slip, and they could be very damaging to the people involved and their families.

We must each treat what is shared in the group as a gift. Act in such a way that they know they can trust you. Should it be discovered that someone in the group has broken this confidence, the group leaders will speak to that person privately, quite possibly asking that he/she not return. Once trust is broken it is almost impossible to restore.

3. Be Considerate

There will be times when one or two do most of the sharing. However, it should not always be the same one or two. If talking comes easily for you, you may need to be careful not to monopolize the conversation. Listen.

When someone is trying to share, there may be long pauses as they collect their thoughts and gather the courage to tell. A comment thrown in at this time may disrupt the flow of their thoughts, and it may be harder for them to have the necessary courage another time. Those who have difficulty sharing need to try to share one small thought. It will be easier the next time.

Be considerate of time. If you have something you want to share be prepared to share it early in the session. After the closing prayer, a short time of visiting may be in order, but be aware that your group leaders may have a busy day ahead.

Be considerate of "old friends". Avoid deserting friends that may not understand all that is happening at this season of your life. When your healing time is over you will want to be friends again. Also, be careful to include everyone in the group in group outings. A group within a group can cause damage to some already hurting people.

Ask that cell phones or other electronic devices be turned off as they are very distracting.

4. Be Sensitive

As people share, there are times when they may need the person beside them to reach out and touch their arm or shoulder. There are also times when they do not want to be touched. Respect their feelings in this area and try to be sensitive to what they need at the time. It is best to let the group leaders take the first step in going to someone or praying with someone.

Give words of encouragement to each other. Part of the dynamics of the group is encouraging each other. There are also times when we need to lovingly challenge each other. As we are each sensitive to each other and to the Holy Spirit, we will flow in loving support. We will also feel the Lord prompting us with encouraging thoughts we can share, and checking us when we should not speak out.

5. Be Accepting

You may have been taught not to feel a certain way, but, as memories long buried come to the surface, so do feelings. It is very important that we realize feelings are not good or bad; they just are. It is what we do with them that makes the difference. If we keep them buried they will destroy us. If we expose them, and deal with them, and let God heal them, we can be set free.

As closed doors are unlocked, strong feelings will come out. As a group, we accept each person as they are with the feelings they are experiencing at the time. Since we cannot make ourselves feel differently, we need God's help. In James 5:16 we are told to *"confess our sins to each other and pray for each other so that we may be healed."* This is the essence of group ministry.

6. Be Willing to Ask for Help

Be considerate of others, but know that you can call someone in the group for prayer when you are having a rough time. You are not alone. God has made us to need others. You may need help one day, but someone else may need your help another day.

7. Be Committed

If bonding is to take place, it will only happen if people are faithful in attendance and in doing the assignments designed to help in the healing journey. Your attendance and participation affect everyone in the group. Don't let other things, even important ones, prevent you from receiving and being a blessing.

Journaling is an avenue for releasing memories, hopes, and feelings. It is an opportunity to express ourselves without fearing another's opinion. It even has physical benefits, as we release the pent up emotions connected to what we are writing, we release some of the stress associated with those feelings.

Decide to memorize Scripture, and do it. The Word of God is given to us to hide in our hearts. It helps us know God, follow His plan for us, and do all He commands us. As we read the Bible, the Scriptures have a cleansing effect on our thoughts and attitudes. They bring us comfort and hope. Praying God's Word is very effective. The more familiar you are with God's Word the more you will bear godly fruit.

Group alone, without Bible reading, church attendance, and journaling, is not enough. If you are serious about this, you will welcome both the encouraging and challenging comments from your leaders. Remember, they are concerned for you, and they love you. Allow God to use them to help you grow.

8. Pray for Your Leaders

They are giving themselves and need your support and prayers. They want you to feel free to call them. All the same, be considerate of their time.

Note: If the leader feels that there is a problem in the group, he/she will talk with the person involved. It may be that individual ministry would be better for now. This does not mean that that person is not loved. Rather, it is a challenge to press forward just a little harder as we keep our eyes on the goal ahead.

Teen Victory's Journey Guidelines

The primary reason for starting a "Teen Victory's Journey" ministry is to prevent years of pain and suffering due to failure to resolve past hurts and to prevent the making of wrong choices. Our goal is to help teens find the joy and purpose God intends for them. In the process they will also find older Christians who care about them, pray for them and will give them godly counsel in a number of areas.

> *Hold on to the pattern of wholesome teaching you learned from me—a pattern shaped by the faith and love that you have in Christ Jesus. Through the power of the Holy Spirit who lives within us, carefully guard the precious truth that has been entrusted to you. - 2 Timothy 1:13-14 (NLT)*

> *Likewise, teach the older women to be reverent in the way they live, not to be slanderers or addicted to much wine, but to teach what is good. [4] Then they can urge the younger women to love their husbands and children, [5] to be self-controlled and pure, to be busy at home, to be kind, and to be subject to their husbands, so that no one will malign the word of God. -Titus 2:3-5*

> *Timothy, my dear son, be strong through the grace that God gives you in Christ Jesus. You have heard me teach things that have been confirmed by many reliable witnesses. Now teach these truths to other trustworthy people who will be able to pass them on to others. - 2 Timothy 2:1-2 (NLT)*

Some Factors to Keep in Mind:

1. These teens are minors. These guidelines must be followed:

   a. A parental consent is a must.

   b. Parents (at least one) must have a good understanding of how the program works, and what the times and locations are.

   c. Parents need to know who will lead the group.

   d. Two leaders should always be present.

   e. A parent should be included in the interview time. One parent needs to sign the Parent Contract and the Parental Consent And Release form.

   f. Safety guidelines should be in place and shared with teens and parents at the interview. These include what will happen if the following occur:

       i. A teen is absent. Parents should encourage them to attend. If they are absent the parents may be called.

Section 3: Preparation For Group Ministry

    ii. They are very emotionally upset and there is concern that they may hurt themselves or others, or that, if they leave, they may be too upset to drive safely, etc.

    iii. An abuse situation needs to be reported.

2. Teens need to be responsible for their own healing. They are to sign the regular contract (page 157). It is helpful if they fill out the "Confidential History" (pages 160-161). They should come to meetings on time and be prepared with pens and Bibles.

3. If parents should ask what is happening the leaders will refer them back to their child. If they are concerned because they are seeing changes, the leaders will work to set up a meeting with parents, the teen, and the leaders.

4. Confidentiality is crucial.

5. The teens are vulnerable and leaders must be aware of subtle group dynamics that could be harmful.

6. A parental permission is also requested to quit the program early.

7. There should be an exit interview with the teen and her parents for the sake of closure.

8. Leaders need to understand that hormones affect them and their moods.

9. Leaders must also be aware that they are not getting into any activities before or after the group that might be detrimental.

10. Leaders need to develop the relationship of a loving mentor, not a good buddy, to gain their respect.

Many of these teens have a very low self-esteem. While our goal is their healing, leaders must keep in mind the fact that this may take some time and some mental reprogramming. They are still young enough that their focus is in the present, and long-term goals seem to belong to another existence. With God's help, miracles can happen for you and for them. Just believe in God and in your group. And remember, these young people will be helped most by an "I know you can!"

Moving On

Teen Victory Journey's Information Card

Name_____   Phone # (   )_____

_____   Date of Birth_____

Father's Name_____

Mother's Name_____

Grade in School_____ If graduated, what year?_____

Name of School_____

School Involvement (activities, etc.)
_____
_____

Do you have a job?_____ If yes,

Where?_____

Hobbies and things you like to do
_____
_____

Goals in life
_____
_____

…being confident of this, that he who began a good
work in you will carry it on to completion
until the day of Christ Jesus.
Philippians 1:6

Section 3: Preparation For Group Ministry

Group Dynamics

Group dynamics involve the actual working of the group process. How does trust develop? What holds people back from active involvement? What fears might they have? How does interaction take place?

Every group in "*Victory's Journey Ministries*" is unique. Every group has its own personality and its own rate of healing. We believe that when God puts a group together there is purpose for that group and its members. Keeping a focus on the "Victory's Journey Progression" helps keep everyone headed in that direction. While reminding the members that they cannot wait until group is winding down to begin working on their healing, allowing the group a certain amount of freedom to develop at its own rate prevents anxiety.

Initial Concerns

Most of those in the group will be nervous about attending the first meeting. In fact one question to ask is, "How do you feel about being here?" Some of them have tried to come up with an excuse not to attend. A few may have succeeded! There are fears of facing the journey, of exposing personal shame, of possible rejection by others, and of being asked to do something they are not ready to do. If the leaders establish a relaxed, but structured, setting at the first meeting, the members will be more comfortable.

Talking about common concerns helps the members to realize they are not alone in their fears. A little laughter goes a long way towards putting people at ease as long as it is not directed at someone. The leaders' warmth sets the tone for acceptance at the very beginning. It may help to remind everyone that others have traveled this road and found hope and healing.

Some frequently heard fears are as follows:

> Will I feel accepted in this group?
>
> Will the others still like me after they know where I've been and what I've done?
>
> Will I be forced into doing something I'm uncomfortable with?
>
> How will they react if I …(get angry, say what I really feel, etc.)?
>
> What if I discover things that I can't handle?
>
> What if someone in the group doesn't keep a confidence?
>
> How will my involvement in group affect my other relationships?

It is good to reassure them that you will be spending the first few weeks mostly getting acquainted and discussing some principles of group ministry. You may have someone who has been healed through the ministry come and share a testimony as this gives hope and encouragement. The leaders will also want to share some of their stories so the group members can get to know them a little better.

Remind the group members that, if after a few weeks they do not feel this is for them, they should talk to you about this.

Interaction/ Common Challenges:

Interaction is based on trust, and that takes time. Some may speak freely, but most will hold back until there is more of a sense of security. Talking about safe and easy subjects in the early meetings helps people start sharing. Remember that even "safe" subjects may trigger a reaction in someone. For example, asking each person to share a happy memory can be difficult for someone who doesn't feel they have any happy memories. Rather than avoiding such issues, allow them to help the group begin the process of deeper sharing and bearing of one another's burdens. If the leader is at ease when things get tough the members will feel more comfortable sharing more painful issues. A caring response will help others develop a caring heart.

One of the reasons for the success of "*Victory's Journey*" is the acceptance and support of those who are hurting and filled with shame. When someone else has similar feelings it says, "I am not alone". When one person shares others find comfort and encouragement, and maybe even solutions, to their own issues. They encourage one another. They pray for one another. A sense of family develops. They truly become united in working together for each other, as well as themselves.

Group members will start to challenge one another. They may pick up something the leaders do not. What started as a leadership responsibility becomes a group responsibility. Honest comments by another group member may be hard to accept, but that is what group is about. Hebrews 10:24 challenges us with these words, *"And let us consider how we may spur one another on toward love and good deeds."* The members are actually learning healthy ways of relating to others. The leaders are still responsible to guide and minister as needed, but they no longer carry the load alone.

Leaders also need to know that when one member challenges another that person may feel uncomfortable, too. They may need some ministry in the days ahead, especially if their words were not well-received.

While some may hold back, it is not uncommon to have a person who monopolizes the sharing time. If the leader doesn't step in at this point others will withdraw. Leaders should also be alert to those who are stuck on current issues, those who are repeatedly sharing the same information, those who make judgment statements, and those who seem to be only centered on themselves. Some may want to talk about their wives or husbands or another person. Remind them that that person is not in group, they are. The group is an opportunity to find personal healing. We must trust God to do the work in another's life while we work on our own pain, our reactions, and our healing.

The best time to note if someone is not fitting into the group relationship is early. By meeting with each member for short personal sessions sometime after the first month, leaders can see how each one feels they are doing and share any concerns for that individual. If there is a problem with one individual he/she will not feel singled out.

If you are having difficulty with someone, ask the Lord for guidance and insights to help you understand why this person is not blending with the others. It may be necessary to spend some time on a one-to-one basis. Feel free to call the ministry leadership for guidance. Is this something that can be worked through? Is this person willing to accept what you are saying? Is he/she willing to make some adjustments?

After speaking to them, pray with them, and if they are willing to work on these areas set up a time to meet again (in two to three weeks). At this time the leaders will need to decide if this person would do better in another area, such as personal ministry.

If someone leaves the group, or is asked to leave, those who are left may feel rejection, loss, and the fear that they will be next. Usually they will understand why this person did not flow with the group, but, because of their own low self-esteem, they may expect to have the same problems. The leaders should allow the opportunity to share feelings and give reassurance. It is very important that the person who has left is not condemned in any way as to do so would destroy trust in the leadership. The leaders can say, "*We are all individuals. "Victory's Journey Ministries" is not the answer for everyone. What works for one person may not be the best for someone else. _____ met with us and we spent some time sharing. The conclusion was that he/she would not be in our group at this time.*"

Ask the group to keep this person in their hearts and their prayers.

As group members begin to share at a more meaningful level, it is important to treat each item shared as a gift from that person to the group. Respect and acceptance of each "gift" helps the one sharing to feel that they are of value, and reduces sharing-related fears in others. The leaders become the role-models in positive group behavior.

Group interaction can be non-verbal, as well as, verbal. Body language, facial expressions, and voice tones carry strong messages. As members learn to develop listening and interactive skills, non-verbal messages should become more open and caring. Leaders should be aware of the body language being communicated by the members and themselves.

As the group bond develops, the members' roles and responsibilities expand. The members begin to reach out to one another in love, support, and, at times, confrontation. The leaders are still there to guide the meeting, but the members now become part of the process of healing. If the groundwork of developing good interaction skills has been laid, this shift will

Moving On

occur naturally.

Giving time to pray together over current needs encourages the members to care about one another beyond the scope of the meeting itself. Stopping a discussion to pray for someone that is having a difficult time cements the idea of carrying each other's burdens in the Lord. Rejoicing together at a victory gives members a little idea of how God rejoices over us.

Difficult Situations

Appropriate behavior is taught and role-modeled early in the group process. As certain standards are held, those in the group will move to meet that standard. For the most part, if the leaders are lax, the group members will be lax; if the leaders hold to high standards, so will their group members. Despite the fact that the leaders have attempted to promote positive and godly behavior, it may still be necessary at times to address a specific issue. When dealing with difficult situations, leaders need to be loving, clear in what they are saying, and positive as to the results of adjusting the said behavior. Avoid negative labeling and embarrassing or hurtful comments. Most people are sensitive and will need reassurance of their worth before and after the issue is dealt with.

Some Specific Situations That Cause Concern Are As Follows:

1. Reluctance to work on personal and group assignments

    A member may fear facing their pains or fear the reactions of the group when these pains are revealed. They may feel such condemnation that it is hard to believe the others in the group could hear their story and not condemn them as they condemn themselves.
Leaders can help the person identify the problem and face their fears.

2. Lack of participation during meetings

    Those who are quiet are often fearful and need to be encouraged and supported. Asking them non-threatening questions may help them to take the first step. Asking for their insights on a Scripture passage that does not have a "right" answer may help them realize their opinions are of value, and so are they. This does need to be addressed as those who are sharing will become anxious about being the only ones giving personal "secrets".

3. Monopolizing the sharing time with personal stories and issues

    The leaders can comment on the fact that this person has a great deal to share and it may be hard to get to the heart of what he/she is really saying. Ask the person to tell the group what he/she really wants to say in one sentence. Ask why the person uses this approach. What are they trying to avoid? Be sensitive to when and how you approach this.

4. Giving so many details that the central thought is lost

Section 3: Preparation For Group Ministry

5. Concentrating on others instead of on their own issues

This person may probe too deeply or give unsought after advice. The leaders may need to limit a question or comment and then refocus. This may be someone who is trying to avoid dealing with their own painful issues.

6. Extreme judgmental behavior or anger towards others

This is often a sign of fear of vulnerability or an effort to prove that they are unlovable. If they will listen to a loving confrontation and deal with these issues they can be guided towards more responsible behavior. Be aware that others may be hurt by their remarks.

7. Those who become too dependent on one or both leaders

Encourage the person to take certain steps on their own before calling. Set limits. Praise independent actions.

8. Those who don't want to deal with issues out of "family loyalty"

Encourage honest and objective statements, rather than "attack" comments. Ask, "What is truth?"

9. Unacceptable talk or behavior

Vulgar or coarse language and behavior grieve the Holy Spirit. Leaders need to role-model godly behavior and speech. If that is not enough, gently comment that we are Christians and everything we say and do should glorify Christ. As we seek to please Christ by our life-styles, He will work in us to bring victory in every area!

10. Cliques

A very special bond will develop among a group who are sharing deep secrets and finding that they are still accepted by each other. They will find themselves drawn to the others in the group. This is healthy, but if they only pray and fellowship with each other, old friends will feel left out and suffer hurts. It will create a negative force in the church.

11. Unnatural bonding

Satan is subtle and the people in your group are vulnerable. During the healing process there may be additional stresses placed on already fragile marital relationships. Families may not be very understanding and supportive.

Those who would pull others from the Lord or from healthy relationships will often present as either very needy or very confident in an area that appeals to the most vulnerable. Be alert and pray for spiritual protection. If you get a sense of concern, do not ignore it. Instead, spend extra time with this person, enhancing your own relationship and continuously pointing the person to God's Word. Someone who is

Moving On

pulling another away from the Lord should also be ministered to, but be wise. Sometimes when you deal with a "perpetrator" the "victim" will see this person as being persecuted by the leaders.

Remember, no situation is hopeless. Healing is a process and it takes time. You may not see changes for a while, but do not give up. With prayer and work, they will come!

Closure

The ending of a group experience brings both joy at what the Lord has done, and a sense of loss at the closing of such intense relationships. Things will be different after group is over, and it is so important that the members are prepared as much as possible.

In one of the last meetings talk about getting together at a special time such as a holiday. Plan what you will do and where you will meet. This will give the security of knowing the group will meet again. Allow enough privacy and time for members to share at this get-together. Encourage the members to expect to have positive testimonies. After all, God is still at work in their lives. They can depend on Him and talk to Him at any time.

Make the last meeting special and positive! You have all worked for months to see them come to this point. It is a day of thanksgiving and celebration. Whatever God has produced in them, it is more than they used to have.

Remind them to pray for one another daily and to keep in touch periodically. Remind them they are still family and siblings grow up and leave home, but if they have had a good relationship, they will always be close. Part of their motivation from this point on will be the knowledge that their brothers/sisters care what happens to them. Even if they do not see each other regularly, they will still be family. Also remind them that the promise of confidentiality still holds. That is one of their love-gifts to one another. Prayer is another gift.

The leaders should contact each person within the month. Occasional notes help them know they are still special to you. And, remember to pray for them.

SECTION 4:
GUIDELINES

Meeting Format

The weekly meeting is the focus of all of the group's interaction. It is very important that the time and place be as consistent as possible. Knowing that a specific time is set aside each week in a "safe" and familiar place gives security. It helps members to know they can make it until the next meeting.

Because structure increases the sense of security, it is important to start on time and have some routine. Always having an opportunity to get a cup of tea or coffee at the beginning helps them know they can count on a few minutes to prepare emotionally. Avoid habitually starting late or running over as this may put added pressure on some members.

Meeting Components:

1. Fellowship Time

We suggest that coffee, tea, and water be available. When people are nervous or stressed it is calming to have something to hold and sip on. The short fellowship time gives the leaders a chance to greet the members separately. Questions about family and health show that all aspects of their lives are of value. It is also a chance to sense where each person is emotionally.

(Snacks are nice but having them every week can create an extra burden for the leaders.)

2. Opening

The opening is the call to "get serious". Singing a chorus or listening to a special song on a tape brings an awareness of the presence of the Lord. Opening in prayer invites the Holy Spirit's help and reminds the group members God is concerned about their needs.

Prayer requests can be taken at this time, but you may find that this can become very time-consuming. Sometimes it is important to do, as family situations can hinder members from concentrating on their healing. You can also ask for the Lord to help each one release their concerns to God, knowing that He is able to meet every need.

3. God's Word

Workbook material is in another script to help you as you teach each lesson. Answers to blanks in the workbook pages are underlined for your ease.

God's Word is vital to the success of "*Victory's Journey*". Without the Bible we have nothing of value to offer. Consider the effect of the Word in these passages:

Moving On

> *Your <u>word</u> is a lamp for my feet and a light on my path. -Psalm 119:105*
>
> *All <u>Scripture</u> is God-breathed and is useful for teaching, rebuking, correcting and training in righteousness, -2 Timothy 3:16*
>
> *For everything that was written in the past was written to teach us, so that through the endurance taught in the <u>Scriptures</u> and the encouragement they provide we might have hope. -Romans 15:4*
>
> *For the <u>word of God</u> is alive and active. Sharper than any double-edged sword, it penetrates even to dividing soul and spirit, joints and marrow; it judges the thoughts and attitudes of the heart.*
> *-Hebrews 4:12*
>
> *Christ loved the church and gave himself up for her to make her holy, cleansing her by the washing with water through the <u>word</u>, and to present her to himself as a radiant church, without stain or wrinkle or any other blemish, but holy and blameless. -Ephesians 5:25b-27*
>
> *Do not conform to the pattern of this world, but be transformed by the renewing of your mind. Then you will be able to test and approve what God's will is--his good, pleasing and perfect will. -Romans 12:2*
>
> *Now what I am commanding you today is not too difficult for you or beyond your reach. No, <u>the word</u> is very near you; it is in your mouth and in your heart so you may obey it.*
>
> *See, I set before you today life and prosperity, death and destruction. For I command you today to love the LORD your God, to walk in obedience to him, and to keep his <u>commands, decrees and laws</u>; then you will live and increase, and the LORD your God will bless you in the land you are entering to possess. -Deuteronomy 30:11,14-16*

What hope there is in the power of God's Word! It produces spiritual fruit (Galatians 5:22,23).

The leaders may occasionally feel impressed to have the sharing from God's Word at the end. However, it can easily be forgotten in a heavy discussion, or someone who really needs it may have to leave early that day. Giving the Scriptures priority seems to set the tone for God to work more freely in hearts. Also, if God has given one of the leaders a specific passage, He has a purpose for it.

4. Meeting Focus

The focus is set in the sharing from the Bible. As the leader follows the lesson guide and workbook, the focus becomes more definite. On occasion, someone from another group may come to share a testimony of hope. (Guests should only be invited if all the group members know in advance.) Leaders should be alert to the group's reactions to what is being shared.

The co-leader should review last week's assignment and ask if it was done. At times, the leader may ask questions related to assignments given the week before or the status of one or more of the members. The leader then presents the lesson and encourages the members to share how they feel about the topics being discussed.

If one member is having a particularly rough time while sharing, it is good for the leaders to go and pray for him/her. Prayer does more than we could ever do in ourselves. God may need to do the supernatural, either as an assurance, or as an answer. Don't be in a hurry, but wait in prayer until there is some kind of release or ministry of the Holy Spirit. As the group develops, the other members may reach out. This is healthy. However, the leaders should always be involved. Because they are leaders, sitting back might be interpreted as not caring.

Often when one shares, others relate to what is shared and the discussion takes off. This is good in that learning is best received when it applies to where we are at the time. Leaders need to be careful, though, that they are following the planned course so that all the steps in the healing process are included. (A lesson can occasionally take two weeks but be careful not to extend the total program too much.)

5. Assignments

Giving specific assignments motivates and increases the level of accountability.

6. Closing

The closing prayer is important as it gives a sense of completion to the session. It serves as a reminder that God will be there to help. No one is alone.

Key Questions Leaders Can Ask During a Meeting:

1. How does that make you feel?
2. What can you do about it?
3. What is the specific thing you feel guilty of?
4. How would you feel if (another member's name, your child) were telling this?
5. Why do you think you feel that way?
6. Can you identify your biggest fear?

Moving On

Special Occasions:

1. Birthdays

Birthdays can be a time to emphasize individual worth and to give an occasional break from the seriousness of the group. Have each one bring a card with a short personal message of encouragement. Cards can be bought or home-made. A special birthday cake adds festivity.

It is good to keep in mind that birthdays may be positive or negative, based on childhood experiences. Someone whose birthday was not celebrated much as a child, may find great joy in being remembered. On the other hand, some may have had their birthdays marked by negative experiences. Remembering such an occasion might be very painful. One possibility is to have a celebration of the date they accepted Christ as their Savior or of the date they chose to join "*Victory's Journey*". As you get to know each member, you will discover what will be helpful or hurtful.

If there are those whose birthdays will not happen during your group experience you can have a party for the whole group. Another option is that the leaders send cards to each person that year.

2. Holidays

Certain holidays can be celebrated with an outing such as a lunch at a local restaurant. A Christmas party is appropriate. Several groups can come together for such an activity if the leaders so choose. Some may be very anxious about this but can grow from the experience. Gift exchanges are nice but the price needs to be limited.

As with birthdays, certain holidays may produce mixed reactions. For any members with a history of involvement in Satanic cults, Halloween is a very fearful time. Cult leaders may even contact them in an attempt to frighten them. Leaders need to be very watchful for signs of depression, regression, and suicidal feelings. Close follow-up is important. Another difficult time is Good Friday and Easter with the emphasis on words such as sacrifice. Be there. Help keep the focus on Jesus, His love and His power. Be prepared to do spiritual warfare. Remind them they will feel better when the season is over.

Holiday breaks are good but do check on your members. Breaks should not be long as some may need the support of the group more at these times. It is best not to miss more than one week at a time.

3. Snow days

Have a system of letting everyone know if group is cancelled due to snow. You might have the group follow a certain school district's lead.

SECTION 5:
LESSON PLANS

WEEK 1:
WHAT ARE YOUR FEELINGS?

As the members arrive, welcome them and introduce them to anyone they may not know. Offer them coffee, tea, or water to drink. Tell them where to hang their coats, where the bathroom is, and any other helpful information that will make them feel more at ease.

Opening Prayer

Thank God for each person and for a time of new beginnings. Do not take prayer requests at this time. If you do, you may find yourself spending a great deal of time on current prayer requests rather than on healing of long-term issues. Pray over all needs represented, and encourage everyone to trust God to handle their cares.

Welcome and Get-Acquainted Time

The first meeting establishes the direction of the group and sets the pattern for interaction and future relationships. If the leaders are comfortable, goal-oriented, and hopeful, these attitudes will transfer to those in the group. It is a good idea to have coffee, tea, and cold water available. This helps the group members to feel more at ease. Kleenex, extra paper, pens, and Bibles are helpful.

Greet the group and invite each to give his/her name and a little about his/her family. Tell them a little about yourselves. Take time to have each member write the other group members' names and information on the chart at the end of this lesson and on page 19 of the workbook. Have them look around the room at one another. Talk about the bonds they will form in the Lord in the coming months. Give a word of caution regarding excluding old friends.

(Note that the change in font shows what material is in their workbook.)

The cheerleaders shout, the fans yell, and everyone is smiling. It's a victory! Whether it's a football game, a race, a spelling bee, or an actual war it is all about winning. A lot depends on that victory. In fact, that victory can alter the course of our futures and possibly the futures of those who come after us. Do you see yourself as a winner?

God, our loving Creator, designed a beautiful blueprint for each of us from the beginning of time. That blueprint is intended to bring us joy and fulfillment if we complete our part in the race of life. We want to be winners, but there is an enemy who wants to stop that from happening. His name is Satan, which means adversary or opponent, and he works hard to defeat God's plans. God wants us to win! His good plans are waiting for us to grab them and move forward in them. Only God knows what will happen if we dare to do just that!

> For I know the plans I have for you," declares the LORD, "plans to prosper you and not to harm you, plans to give you hope and a future. - Jeremiah 29:11

Workbook Introduction

"Victory's Journey" is a ministry dedicated to helping emotionally and spiritually wounded people find healing. This program is usually done as a small group healing ministry, but it can also be used individually or as discipleship training. Whatever format you choose, I would like to welcome you as you begin the journey toward the joy God has for you. You may have asked the questions, "How can I have joy? How can I fix my broken heart, broken dreams, broken life"? I want to encourage you that God knows your situation. He understands your pain, rejection, fear, shame, and sorrow. He asks you to follow Him and be totally His, just as you are, even with the pain of all of your past hurt. Take "the victory journey", and look forward to what He has for you. It is good!

Ask, "What do you want God to do for you in this group?"

Talk about the key verse, purpose and motto of Victory's Journey. Read the key verse together.

Key Verse

> Being confident of this, that he who began a good work in you will carry it on to completion until the day of Christ Jesus. - Philippians 1:6

Our Purpose

Jesus Christ offers abundant life, and it is God's desire to see His sons and daughters enjoy the life He gives. He wants us to be all we can be in Him. His Word has so many promises for those who follow His ways. Here are a few for you to hold on to during this journey. We suggest you write them on cards and carry them with you until they become a part of your thought patterns.

> You have made known to me the paths of life; you will fill me with joy in your presence. - Acts 2:28

> For I know the plans I have for you," declares the Lord, "plans to prosper you and not to harm you, plans to give you hope and a future. - Jeremiah 29:11

Motto: "Look and Live"

What does that say to you? Does it give you hope?

God wants us to face our pain, to look at it. It is a part of our history and ignoring it will only *produce more pain. When we identify the thing that holds us back we can really give it to Jesus. Letting go and trusting our loving God allows us to live the abundant life Jesus promised to all His followers in John 10:10.*

Tell your new Victory's Journey members that we believe that in this small group atmosphere of acceptance and confidentiality, they will find the freedom to look at their pain and then deal with it according to Scriptural principles.

The purpose of the first week's meeting is to help you look forward. The key to success is setting goals and staying focused on completing them. It can be beneficial to write God a letter telling Him what you hope to gain from this journey.

This will not be an easy journey. To find healing we do have to face issues and that can be hard. As you face some hard issues, you may feel anxious, discouraged, and fearful. Feel free to contact one of your leaders for prayer and direction. If you are doing this on your own, find a strong Christian who can be there when you need to talk to someone. Remember that you are already a survivor and that God will always be there for you.

Group Guidelines   (page 37; page 12 in the workbook)

Discuss each person's responsibilities as you review the guidelines. Suggest that they follow along in their workbooks and take notes as you cover the basic guidelines of the group. Even though the "Group Guidelines" were covered in the initial interview, they need to be covered in detail at the first meeting. They will need to be reviewed again the following week and again the next month.

When you have gone over the guidelines, ask if there are any questions or suggestions for other guidelines.

The Victory Journey's Progression (page 13; page 14 in the workbook)

Contract

Review the contract they signed at their interview, especially the confidentiality paragraph. (The leaders are encouraged to sign the contract in the group's presence.) There is a statement which each one signed that states he/she read the contract and understands that the "Victory's Journey Ministries" leaders are volunteer lay persons who are sharing Scriptural principles as friends and not as mental health professionals. Because the leaders are not professional counselors, they may on occasion need to consult with the leadership of "Victory's Journey", a pastor, or a mental health professional. In the contract, he/she agrees that the leaders may seek such direction should they become concerned regarding his/her well-being or the well-being of another person(s). (This would be done in a way that was felt to be to his/her best interest.)

Confidentiality stands even if someone leaves a group.

Moving On

God's Word

You, as leaders, are involved in this ministry because you believe it will provide the tools they need to find the healing they need. They will receive from this class what they put into it. This is a good time to let the new members know that you are expecting God to do a beautiful work in their lives as they do their part.

The problems in your life are a big deal to God. Because He cares so much, He has led you to this place and to this time. Know that you are beginning a journey with a special group of people. As the journey continues, you will get to know a lot about each other, you will mourn and laugh together, and you will pray for one another. As God heals your hurts from the past (or present) you will be free to be all He has planned for you to be.

This journey involves dealing with areas of pain that you have not totally faced before. God, in His love, gives humans the ability to "turn off" certain areas of memory until they are able to deal with them. But if you do not deal with these feelings they will surface in other areas of life. This can result in times of uncontrollable anger or an inability to cope with seemingly small matters. You may live in a heavy fog of depression, unable to be all you feel God wants you to be, but not sure why.

Yes, you can ignore the pain or you can go back prayerfully and begin the process. James 5:16 and 1 John 1:9 speak of confession as a step towards freedom and healing. That is your part. For, as you look at your pain and share it with others who care, you can learn to walk in the freedom God has made available through the cross. God desires to give you abundant life. It is yours if you will only "look and live!"

No pain is too small; no pain is too big. Both can prevent us from being all God intends us to be. If you are here, your pain is significant. It is affecting your life and needs to be dealt with. Yet God has the power to work in you more than you can even imagine because it is His power that is at work (Ephesians 3:20). Invite Him to search your heart. He will lead you.

Joy is a gift of gladness that your loving Heavenly Father wants to give you in a measure so full you cannot contain all of it. This joy was bought for you with the precious blood of Jesus, God's Son. To have this gift we must be in Christ (John 17:16-26). We must receive Jesus, His gift of forgiveness from our sinfulness, and His teachings. As we allow God to be Lord of every aspect of our lives, He takes our pain and replaces it with His love, peace, and joy.

In the middle of your everyday life, God calls you aside to hear His voice. In Isaiah 51:3 we learn that the Lord comforts and has compassion on your place of ruins. He promises to make the wasted land like the Garden of Eden, a place of joy and song. His desire, according to Song of Solomon 2:4, is to take you into the banquet hall of His presence and pour blessings on you! Joel 2:25 is a promise of restoration for wasted years.

Week 1: What Are You Feeling?

Please take time to write a prayer to God using the following Scripture:

> *The LORD will surely comfort Zion and will look with compassion on all her ruins; he will make her deserts like Eden, her wastelands like the garden of the LORD. Joy and gladness will be found in her, thanksgiving and the sound of singing. - Isaiah 51:3*

Look at the following Bible passage. What promises do you have as you begin?

> *But now, this is what the LORD says-- he who created you, Jacob, he who formed you, Israel: "Do not fear, for I have redeemed you; I have summoned you by name; you are mine.*
>
> *When you pass through the waters, I will be with you; and when you pass through the rivers, they will not sweep over you. When you walk through the fire, you will not be burned; the flames will not set you ablaze. For I am the LORD, your God, the Holy One of Israel, your Savior - Isaiah 43:1-3*

God's Word promises us in Isaiah 43:1-3 that even though we will pass through some rivers, some waters, and some fire, God is with us. Problems and conflicts need to be dealt with, and that means going through them instead of around them. It means allowing ourselves to feel the pain so that we can release it to Jesus. The promise is that we can come through the waters and the fire in hope and victory.

This journey will take hard work and determination, but if you do your part you will see the promised hope and restoration. At times you may be tempted to give up, but in those hard times remember that others have taken this journey and made it through to the healing power of Jesus Christ. You can do it too!

Make this verse your prayer:

> *Search me, O God, and know my heart; test me and know my anxious thoughts. See if there is any offensive way in me, and lead me in the way everlasting. - Psalm 139:23-24*

Meeting Focus

Feelings, Thoughts, and Actions

Some people say they don't have feelings. Others are very aware of their feelings. Let's talk about feelings, thoughts and actions. What are they?

Moving On

Feelings -

Thoughts -

Actions -

Feelings *are not good or bad, they just are. Some examples are sadness, joy, anger, fear, peace, and hope. A feeling is a sense of comfort or of discomfort.*

Can you think of a feeling you have had that was positive and made you feel good?

What about one that made you feel very uncomfortable?

While feelings are just emotions, if we do not deal with negative feelings they can grow into roots of bitterness and strongholds of the enemy that will hurt us later.

Thoughts *are impressions on the mind. We have a choice of what we will think about. What should we think about in Philippians 4:8?*

What can thoughts and meditations produce?

> *My heart grew hot within me, while I meditated, the fire burned; then I spoke with my tongue: - Psalm 39:3*

This verse states that thoughts (meditations) can ignite feelings, and in the end produce actions such as speech. We are responsible for the choices we make, even in our thought-life.

Actions *are the physical or outward speech or behavior that comes from our hearts and thoughts.*

> *For out of the heart come evil thoughts, murder, adultery, sexual immorality, theft, false testimony, slander. - Matthew 15:19*

Have you ever met someone who acted on feelings alone? How comfortable were you around that person? What is the best pattern to follow?

F – T – A

As we give God permission to search our hearts and know our thoughts, He will help us deal with what we need to deal with and help us to find true victory!

God began a good work in you, and you can be sure it is His intent to complete the job. That is encouraging. God is for you, and He is working with you and in you as you yield to Him. He is not mean or harsh, but He does need us to trust and obey if we are to fulfill our purpose. As we do, even the worst situations can become a blessing. Why? Because Jesus lives in us!

Ask them how they feel about being at the first meeting. What are their fears and expectations? Ask if it was difficult to come. Most probably did not want to come, but they are here. That involved making a good choice, despite feelings such as anxiety. Just being here shows a desire to see a more abundant life.

This is an opportunity to help the members develop realistic expectations. As they face the hard issues in their lives, they will face many emotions or feelings. You want them to know they can contact either leader for prayer and direction. The leaders will share the information and pray together for them. Remind them that you will be there to help them through the hard times. Most importantly, God will be there. He will not fail them.

Those in the group have chosen to be involved in a ministry of godly support and healing. That is good. The enemy will try to discourage them by tempting them with negative thoughts. It is their choice what thoughts they allow to affect their feelings and their actions. (Philip. 4:8)

F-T-A is the best pattern. We should always think before we act.

Next Week's Assignment

1. Bring a journal. Also, decide where to keep it at home. You may start writing some early memories or thoughts about being in the group. You might want to write about any uncertainties you have.

This is a good place to discuss the importance of having a journal. Feelings and thoughts can be very vague. It is hard to deal with vague issues. Writing our feelings and thoughts clarifies them and helps us face them. It also helps us take the hurts and fears out of our hearts so we can "look and live". Praying before writing invites the Holy Spirit to guide our thoughts. The journaling can be done as "Dear God" letters. Afterwards we place our written feelings and thoughts into His hands.

2. Begin to memorize Philippians 1:6.

Remember, there will be times when you would rather stay home. It is important that you make the commitment to be here, regardless of how anxious you may feel. This is part of the healing process, and it will get easier.

Workbook pages should be done weekly. Assignments make us think, dig into God's Word, and deal with issues that we might avoid otherwise. Those who do journaling and assignments will grow more rapidly than those who do not.

They may be tempted to look ahead. That is not helpful. We need to allow the lessons to build one on another. Looking ahead can be overwhelming.

Let them know that you are available to them. Before contacting you, they should pray, journal, and praise God for all He is about to do. It is really the Holy Spirit, the Great Comforter, who will lead them to victory!

Closing Prayer

Establish that God is the Source of our hope and help. If you like, take prayer requests at this time. Pray for each one by name.

Do not encourage them to stay too long as that is not a good precedent to establish.

If the leaders have doubts regarding a member's ability to flow with the group, they should talk to him/her in the next few weeks. Ask how he/she views his/her role in the group now and in the future. What fears do they have? Be honest about any uncertainties you have. Scheduling a "chat" with each member of the group may allow them to express themselves more freely on a one-on-one basis. Some may need an extra touch of reassurance.

Before the group members get into sharing at a deeper level, make them aware of the need to be sure this is the direction they want to take at this time. It is possible that some did not fully understand the purpose or that they now realize they are not ready to work on these concepts. For whatever the reason, there is no condemnation in leaving the group. Nor does leaving the group now mean that someone cannot be in a group at a later date. What is important is the fact that anyone who is leaving should do so before the others in the group have shared too many personal details of their life stories. It's unfair to receive information unless they're committing to this friendship.

Week 1: What Are You Feeling?

Leaders and Group Members:

NAME	PHONE & E-MAIL ADDRESS	ADDRESS

Note: Confidentiality stands, even if you should leave the group.

Prayer Requests:

WEEK 2:
WHAT IS PAIN

Review the motto and guidelines.

Have them each do a "Personal Evaluation".

This is a self-test used simply to create an awareness of need. When they complete the evaluations have them put them in envelopes you provide and seal them. You will open them at the end of the group so they can each see what God has done. Suggest that they be kept in the member's workbook. Teens should let the leaders keep them.

God's Word

Did you ever smash your finger in a car door or break your big toe? I can still remember when the groomsmen kidnapped me right after my wedding. They pushed me into the back seat of a two-door car and I put my foot on the front seat (which was folded forward) to support myself. Just that quickly someone sat on that seat and as the seat back came down on my big toe there was a pop. It hurt! I not only saw stars; they danced in front of me. Now I know that no one intended to hurt me, but I had to fix the problem with a splint to allow that toe to heal. Our pains in life need a "fix".

Why is it necessary to look at past pains? Because unresolved pain leads to bigger issues. The pain in my toe isn't as severe today because I have already survived the initial incident, and healing took place. As each one of us looks at our past pain, we can find healing and abundant life. Jesus is waiting to help work through the process. You can succeed because of His great power at work in you and because of the support of those who really care.

Our key verse is Philippians 1:6, "being confident of this, that he who began a good work in you will carry it on to completion until the day of Christ Jesus". Read it and think about what God has done in your life to grow you and complete you. The One who began the good work in you at your salvation has many more good things in store. Try to say Philippians 1:6 by memory. How confident are you that Jesus is going to do a complete and a good work in you?

Read the key verse, Philippians 1:6, together.

Meeting Focus

Teach "What is Pain?" and allow time for discussion and sharing. Some will relate to one, or more, of the types of abuse, and may need personal ministry or a touch on the shoulder. It is always alright to stop for prayer if you see someone really struggling.

An onion is an excellent example of how God wants to peel back the layers and let the tender core of our beings reflect His love. The peeling process often brings tears, but tears bring

Moving On

release. Also God doesn't peel the layers back roughly. He knows when and where each person is feeling safe and most ready. There is often a little bit of green in the very center, reminding us that there is life after pain and tears.

As you read through the following section have them follow in their workbooks.

What is Pain?

Everybody carries some junk in their backpack that they really don't need. Whether big or small, that junk weighs us down and keeps us from being all that God wants us to be. You matter to God! The problems you face are a big deal to Him because He cares so much for you, even if you do not feel that way right now. In fact, He cares so much He has led you to this time and this place so that you could find healing in His love.

In dealing with the healing of past pain, we need to identify past and pain. The past is anything <u>before</u> today. It can be from your childhood or from later in your life. Pain is something that has caused you to <u>suffer</u>. That suffering cripples you and prevents you from being all that God intended you to be.

Don't say, "My pain is too little to mention." If you are affected by it, it needs to be healed so you can move on in your life. Don't say, "My pain is too big for God to do anything." God says in Ephesians 3:20 that He "is able to do immeasurably more than all we ask or imagine, according to his power that is at work within us." It is not the size of the pain, but the <u>reactions</u> that pain has caused in your life that matter.

Different people react differently to pain. That can be a way of coping. God gives us the ability to shut down areas of emotion and memory when we are not able to deal with the distress. There may be whole blocks of time that seem to be missing in a person's life. The person knows something is wrong but may not be sure what it is. Other people know what happened but have shut down any emotional response. After a while they find they have difficulty even feeling good feelings. Some people wear "masks". At first this helps to cope with the hurt, but in time these masks become walls to hide behind. Often hurting people just don't know how to come out into freedom.

Others ignore the pains of the past. If we deny or ignore the past pain we can end up stuck under a heavy fog of depression or anger, unable to be all we feel God wants us to be. Ignored pain does not go away. Instead, it becomes like a cooking pot on a hot fire that is not watched. The pressure keeps building until the lid pops off, leaving a mess. Pain that is not dealt with will find another way out, and it will often hurt someone else. It is so much better to go back prayerfully and be healed.

One of the first steps in the healing process is to identify the pain.

There are five types of pain. They are as follows:

1. Physical - severe illness or injury to yourself or a loved one. It may be abusive. This can

Week 2: What Is Pain?

include threats. It also includes bullying by someone bigger or stronger or more powerful.

2. *Spiritual -*

   A. *Disappointment – someone you looked up to failed you. Therefore you see God as failing you, and you cannot trust Him.*

   B. *Past or current sins (Rebellion leads to deception.)*

3. *Emotional – hurtful relationships and rejection (includes death, departure of a loved one). Usually there is a feeling of never being good enough to make a loved one stay. Insecurity is an issue.*

4. *Negligence – abandonment, lack of proper care and provision. This can include the pain of a parent who did not stop abuse.*

5. *Sexual (may be subtle or suggestive) – any violation of privacy in the sexual area. This can include being forced to watch another person, touching in the private areas, and sexual intercourse.*

Sexual abuse always produces <u>guilt</u> to the victim. God made us to feel pleasure when certain areas are touched. A child feels guilty if they enjoyed these sensations. There is a violation of the conscience. The abuser often makes the child feel that they are to blame.

Abusers seek out vulnerable victims. Some of them want help, but they don't know how to get it. They are afraid of losing their reputation. They need God, too.

Why do we need to look at past pain? Because pain that is unresolved leads to problems. Headaches and illnesses can result from blocked pain.

(Mention that there can be other causes for these physical problems.)

Marital conflicts, even passed on abuse, are not uncommon. The spouse and children may become secondary victims.

God wants to heal you. He made you very special and He has a good plan for your life.

Look at the following verses. What key truths stand out to you?

> *For you created my inmost being; you knit me together in my mother's womb. I praise you because I am fearfully and wonderfully made;- Psalm 139:13-14*

> *"For I know the plans I have for you," declares the Lord, "plans to prosper you and not to harm you, plans to give you hope and a future." - Jeremiah 29:11*

Satan, our enemy, wants to stop us from being the person God plans for us to be. He wants us to hurt and pass the hurt on. The choice is ours. The process of healing is not easy and it may take time, but if we are willing to start, God will be there to help us.

Moving On

The journey starts as we confess our pain, our shame, and our own sins to Jesus. (1 John 1:9). He forgives us and cleanses us. Then as we allow Him to search our hearts and open us up to His love and grace, as we share our hurts with those who truly care, and as we begin to grow in God's ways, the healing will happen!

A good prayer to remember is Psalm 139:23, "Search me, God, and know my heart."

Ask, "How can we be more open to the Holy Spirit's flashlight?"

- Noticing how we feel when we act in certain ways (Is the Holy Spirit convicting us?)

- Having an accountability partner

- Meditating on our Bible reading of the day and journaling on verses God prompts us to reread

- Asking the Lord to help us be more aware of where we are spiritually

Next Week's Assignment

1. Take time to think about who God is. Write your thoughts in your journal. Do the page in your workbook, "Who is God?"

2. Pray every day for each one in the group. Ask God to help all of you to do the assignments and journaling.

Closing

Hand each man, a "Letter to the Wife". There is also a letter to a friend.

Ask each one to pray daily for the leaders and other members in the group.

Pray for each person in the group individually. Leaders need to be careful that both leaders give each member equal attention. Close in prayer.

Week 2: What Is Pain?

Who is God?

Look up the following verses and see how God is described:

Jehovah-Jireh = _____ Genesis 22:14

Jehovah-Rapha = _____ Exodus 15:22-26

Jehovah-Tsidkenu = _____ Jeremiah 33:14-16

Jehovah-Shammah = _____ Ezekiel 48:35

What does God promise in the following Scriptures?
    Psalm 27:9-10
    John 14:16-18
    Hebrews 13:5

What can you do when you feel God is not there for you? (see 1 Chron. 28:9, Jer. 33:3, 1John 5:14-15)

Who is God? (Look up God's characteristics in your concordance)

WEEK 3:
WHO IS GOD? - PART 1

It might be a good time to take some short prayer requests.

Ask everyone to bring out their journals, close them, and place them on a table. Have a time of prayer over the journals that the Lord will help each member to feel the Lord's freedom and healing as their writing begins to reveal deeper truths.

Meeting Focus

Discuss feelings. Remind them that feelings are neither *good nor bad*; they just *are*.

Many of us get upset about certain things and then wonder why we react the way we do. Our reactions are frequently linked to two things – our past pain and our current expectations. It is important that each of us looks at our issues realistically if we want to be healed. It is in looking at them that they can be dealt with.

What is something that bothers you?

Why does it bother you?

Some common excuses for not dealing with issues are:

1. "It was so long ago. Why bother?" What does Hebrews 4:13 say?

2. "I can't tell God." What does Psalm 139:3 say?

3. "No one will believe me." What does Jeremiah 17:10 say?

4. "Nothing will change." What does John 8:32 say?

Many people are hurting. They say, "I'm fine" but much of who they are is affected by things they are trying to forget. Denying or minimizing is an example. It is a form of hiding. Adam and Eve hid from God and then cast blame. David covered up his adultery and murder, but it still had to be dealt with. Peter was afraid of the consequences if he admitted to being with Jesus, so he denied Him. We do not want to deny or minimize our feelings. Instead, we need to bring them into the light of God's love so we can deal with them and put them under the blood of Jesus where they can no longer destroy us. Jesus has helped you to this point, and He wants to completely heal you. He is there with you in the darkest time.

> "Though the mountains be shaken and the hills be removed, yet my unfailing love for you will not be shaken nor my covenant of peace be removed," says the Lord, who has compassion on you. - Isaiah 54:10

Feelings that are not dealt with will come out in other ways, such as physical symptoms, emotional disorders, or behavioral problems. Fear, moodiness, shame, relationship difficulties, vulnerability, and negative self-talk are only a few of the problems that can come from repressed pain. It is as you share your hurts that you can be all God wants you to be. In fact, there is a definite relationship between the amount of sharing and unloading a person does, and the amount of healing received. While it is painful to share, it is much more hurtful to hold in pain or shame. In the group, each person will learn to accept their feelings and those of others. Then they can learn to release the pain and be free of feelings that are destructive.

Journaling is very important. It can help you get a better understanding of why you feel the way you do. Just getting started can be tough, but remember, you can be creative in your journaling. Try writing letters to God, drawing pictures (even if they are stick figures), and making collages.

Share how journaling has helped you. Journaling can be in the form of a letter to God, a drawing, a collage, or just writing what you are feeling. It will probably be very difficult to get started writing in the journals. A good beginning is to write about the reasons each one felt a need to be in the "*Victory's Journey Ministries*". Other early topics can include feelings at the first few meetings, early memories (happy or sad), the first house(s) a person remembers, and people who played a significant role in early childhood memories.

You can allot ten minutes in class to writing in journals. (Setting a timer will let them know it will only be ten minutes.) Ask if anyone would like to share what they have written or how they felt about writing.

God's Word

Begin teaching Section I of "Our Relationship With God, Our Parent". Encourage the members to share their views and what they wrote about who God is. Pause if necessary to allow someone to share how this affects them. Encourage everyone to share their perception of God. For some, this may be based on a hurtful relationship with a person who failed them.

With each Scripture passage you study, encourage the group to share what the Lord has shown them before you share your thoughts. You might want to take the passage verse by verse or paragraph by paragraph. Remind them that this is not a Bible study, as such, but a discussion of Scriptural principles that help us make the journey from pain to peace.

Our relationship with God, our Parent

1. Who is God?

He is the Almighty Creator, the Holy One, the King of Kings. Do you think of Him as near or far away? Think about God as a parent. Repeatedly He tells us this is who He is.

How does that make you feel?

Week 3: Who is God? - Part 1

God does not equate with an earthly parent, not even a good one. The Bible pictures God for us as the perfect parent! He fathered you. He is your strong foundation and security. When He gave you birth He had a desire for you to be His child.

In Deuteronomy 32:18 God says,

> "You deserted the Rock, who fathered you; you forgot the God who gave you birth."

In Isaiah 9:6, He is always there for you.

> "For to us a child is born, to us a son is given, and the government will be on his shoulders. And he will be called Wonderful Counselor, Mighty God, Everlasting Father, Prince of Peace."

Matthew 6:8-9 tells us He cares for each of us and our needs.

> Do not be like them, for your Father knows what you need before you ask him. 'This, then, is how you should pray: 'Our Father in heaven..'" (shows established relationship)

How do we become His children?

> You are all sons of God through faith in Christ Jesus,- Galatians 3:26 (NASB)

John 1:12-13 tells us we must receive Jesus and believe in His Name:

> Yet to all who did receive him, to those who believed in his name, he gave the right to become children of God-- children born not of natural descent, nor of human decision or a husband's will, but born of God. - John 1:12-13

How do we live as God's children?

> Therefore, brothers and sisters, we have an obligation--but it is not to the flesh, to live according to it. For if you live according to the flesh, you will die; but if by the Spirit you put to death the misdeeds of the body, you will live, for those who are led by the Spirit of God are the children of God. The Spirit you received does not make you slaves, so that you live in fear again; rather, the Spirit you received brought about your adoption to sonship. And by him we cry, "Abba, Father". The Spirit himself testifies with our spirit that we are God's children. Now if we are children, then we are heirs--heirs of God and co-heirs with Christ, if indeed we share in his sufferings in order that we may also share in his glory. - Romans 8:12-17

Verse 13 says we have an obligation. This is not condemnation (Rom 8:1), but the willingness to be open to conviction because we want to please Him. To please Him we need His help. Our part is being willing to start on the path to victory.

Satan wants to use fear to control you. Verses 15 and 16 tells us that fear is not God's will for you. He does not want you to be a slave to fear. Children should not need to live in fear of their parents.

Moving On

The witness in our spirits that we are indeed God's children is given by the Holy Spirit.

How does He do that?

In verse 17 we see that the life of following Jesus and being a child of God may include suffering. It is not always an easy road but there is a promise. You are an heir of eternal life! It is not for what you can get but because you love Him. (Remember He first loved you.)

Job really had a powerful faith in His Father God. What did he say in Job 13:15?

> "Though He slay me, yet I will hope in him;" - Job 13:15

Next Week's Assignment

1. *Check out what God is like according to the Bible, using your concordance.*

2. *Keep on journaling and praying for one another.*

WEEK 4:
WHO IS GOD? - PART 2

God's Word

What did you learn about what the Bible says about God? Our relationship with God is based on His Word, not what we feel. While feelings are very important, truth in Jesus is what sets us free. Allow the Scriptures we look at in this group to penetrate deeply into your spirit. There is great power in absorbing and meditating on what God says to us.

My father was a great example of God's love. I knew the rules but I also knew he loved me unconditionally. My mother loved me and I knew it, but her scolding and criticism contributed to my feeling that I wasn't as good as I should be. The result was I knew God loved me unconditionally, BUT I had a hard time believing that He enjoyed me just because I was His child. 1 John 4:16-18 taught me that as I became secure in my love relationship with my Heavenly Father I could begin to expect His favor over my life. That brought so much freedom!

How we view a parent can affect how we view God. How do you view your father? ... your mother? Can you see a relationship to how you view God? This might be a good time to journal on your relationship with your father or mother.

Our relationship with God, our Parent *(continued)*

   2. How does God "parent" us?

Deuteronomy 1:31 says He <u>carries</u> us.

> *"... in the wilderness. There you saw how the Lord your God <u>carried you, as a father carries his son, all the way you went until you reached this place.</u>"*

In Isaiah 49:15 He reminds us that even if our earthly parents may <u>forget</u> us, He will not:

> *"Can a mother forget the baby at her breast and have no compassion on the child she has borne? Though she may forget, <u>I will not forget you!</u>*

Isaiah 66:13 tells us when we hurt, He <u>comforts</u> us.

> *As a mother comforts her child, <u>so will I comfort you;</u>*

This wonderful God also <u>takes great delight</u> in us. He quiets our spirit with His love, as we rest in Him. This gives us the picture of a parent rocking their child.

Moving On

Zephaniah 3:17 says:

> "The Lord your God is with you, the Mighty Warrior who saves. <u>He will take great delight in you; in his love he will no longer rebuke you,</u> but will rejoice over you with singing."

He enjoys giving us good <u>gifts</u> according to Matthew 7:11:

> *If you, then, though you are evil, know how to give good gifts to your children, how much more will <u>your Father in heaven give good gifts to those who ask him!</u>*

Remember that good gifts to God are not necessarily material gifts.

In Luke 13:34 He <u>gathers</u> us close to Himself:

> *<u>....., how often I have longed to gather your children together, as a hen gathers her chicks under her wings,</u> but you were not willing!*

Meditate on God as a parent.

Are you allowing Him to be all He wants to be in your life? *(Our lack of trust can hold back the flow of God's blessings.)*

How do you feel about God being your Father?

We must be willing to put our past ideas/concepts of a parent, or father, behind us and reach toward what God's Word says He is!

Here are seven simple steps to knowing who God is according to His Word:

1. <u>Confess</u> the Word of God as totally true.

2. <u>Believe</u> on Jesus Christ and ask Him to forgive your sins. Decide to follow Jesus in all the areas of your life.

3. <u>Praise</u> God for who He is and what He has done, and is doing, in your life.

4. <u>Reject</u> Satan's lies.

5. <u>Pray and read</u> the Bible, and think about what it is saying to you.

6. <u>Act</u> on what the Word says to do.

7. <u>Fellowship</u> with other believers in a Bible-teaching church.

Week 4: Who Is God? - Part 2

Maybe you have a handle on the fact that God loves you, but you fear His discipline. God does not want you to live in fear. After all, He loves you. But sometimes discipline is necessary to guide us in the right way. If we obey God's gentle nudges He will not have to give harder prods! If He does have to discipline us He knows what we need and is there to help us.

> *And have you completely forgotten this word of encouragement that addresses you as a father addresses his son? It says,*
>
> *"My son, do not make light of the Lord's discipline, and do not lose heart when he rebukes you, because the Lord disciplines those he loves, and he chastens everyone he accepts as his son." - Hebrews 12:5-6*

Remember..

> *...the Lord is good and his love endures forever; his faithfulness continues through all generations. - Psalm 100:5*

3. What is our role in the relationship?

God proved His character to the children of Israel. He made promises to Abraham and to Moses and He kept His promises. He took them out of Egypt, He led them through the wilderness, He supplied their every need, and He never left them. Israel's reaction to all this was that in every trial they cried, "I want to go back to Egypt". They were so busy complaining about what they didn't like that it seems they hardly noticed all the miracles!

What could they have focused on instead?

What is your focus?

They easily went back to their idols. They easily gave up. They forgot their God, the One who loved them, fathered them, carried them, provided for them, and would always be willing to be there for them. They even made a golden calf and worshipped it!

What idols get between us and our relationship with our Heavenly Father?

Idols can be thoughts and actions.

They can be bitterness, rebellion, greed, addictions, other activities or relationships - anything that grieves the Holy Spirit!

Joshua had been there through the long wilderness journey. Moses was dead and the responsibility of leadership into the Promised Land was his. What did God say to Joshua?

Read Joshua 1:1-9. Note the points that are underlined here:

Moving On

> *<u>After the death of Moses</u> the servant of the Lord, the Lord said to Joshua son of Nun, Moses' aide: "Moses my servant is dead. Now then, you and all these people, get ready to cross the Jordan River into the land I am about to give to them--to the Israelites. I will give you every place where you set your foot, as I promised Moses. Your territory will extend from the desert to Lebanon, and from the great river, the Euphrates--all the Hittite country--to the Mediterranean Sea in the west. No one will be able to stand against you all the days of your life. As I was with Moses, so I will be with you; I will never leave you nor forsake you.*
>
> *"<u>Be strong and courageous,</u> because you will lead these people to inherit the land I swore to their ancestors to give them. <u>Be strong and very courageous. Be careful to obey all the law</u> my servant Moses gave you; do not turn from it to the right or to the left, that you may be successful wherever you go. Keep this Book of the Law always on your lips; <u>meditate on it day and night</u>, so that you may be careful to do everything written in it. Then you will be prosperous and successful. Have I not commanded you? <u>Be strong and courageous. Do not be afraid do not be discouraged, for the Lord your God will be with you wherever you go.</u>" - Joshua 1:1-9*

This Scripture applies to every Christian. What is your part in your relationship with God?

There were more promises from God, but ... Joshua had to do his part to receive those promises. He did and we read that God was with him as He promised.

However, as Joshua neared the end of his life there was a question that had to be settled. In the twenty-fourth chapter of Joshua we see that he assembled all the tribes to present themselves to God. Joshua reminded them of all God had done for them, and then came the ultimate decision, the big choice.

> *"Now fear the LORD and serve him with all faithfulness. Throw away the gods your ancestors worshiped beyond the Euphrates River and in Egypt, and serve the LORD. But if serving the LORD seems undesirable to you, then choose for yourselves this day whom you will serve, whether the gods your ancestors served beyond the Euphrates, or the gods of the Amorites, in whose land you are living. But as for me and my household, we will serve the LORD." - Joshua 24:14-15*

We MUST choose... each of us for ourselves. Who will you serve? Who will you follow in your thoughts, words and actions? Who will be your God? What choices can you make that will help you to heal?

You may want to pray, addressing God as "Daddy". That is Scriptural (Romans 8:15).

Practice praying to your Loving Father this week.

Meeting Focus

How we view a parent can affect how we view God. How did each person view their mother? …their father?

Can they see a relationship to their view of God? Ask the members to share from their journaling.

Take time to pray and to minister as the Holy Spirit leads you.

Close by praying the Lord's Prayer together in a loving tone.

WEEK 5:
THE POWER OF GOD'S WORD

God's Word

If possible, have someone from an earlier group come and share a testimony of what God has done in his/her life. It is important that the sharing be specific as this establishes a pattern of openness for the new group's dynamics. However, it is also important that the emphasis be on the healing, not the pain. The guest might share some personal experiences with journaling, such as any anxieties he/she felt and truths that were learned. Allow time for questions and discussion. This is also a good time for the leaders to share some Scriptures that helped them push towards their healing.

God's Word is very important in our lives and in our healing. The Scriptures affect us in a number of ways. Reading Scripture helps us to know what God wants us to be and do. It is powerful in purifying our minds, in healing our hurts, and in helping us to walk closer to the Lord. What are some ways God can help us through His Word?

Discuss the following verses:

The Word gives wisdom, guidance, encouragement, rebuke, and hope! The Bible is a gift that can help us in healing and walking with the Lord:

> *But whenever anyone turns to the Lord, the veil is taken away. Now the Lord is the Spirit, and where the Spirit of the Lord is, there is freedom. And we all, who with unveiled faces all contemplate the Lord's glory, are being transformed into his image with ever-increasing glory, which comes from the Lord, who is the Spirit. - 2 Corinthians 3:16-18*

The veil in this passage clouds our understanding. If we allow God to remove it we can see God's truths and it will be reflected in our lives. God's Word is true. It stands when other ideas and helps fail. Reading it has a cleansing effect on our thought patterns.

> *Sanctify them by the truth; your word is truth. - John 17:17*
>
> *…make her holy, cleansing her by … the word, - Ephesians 5:26*

Do you struggle with past guilt and shame? What tool has God given us to make us clean and even holy?

> *I have hidden your word in my heart that I might not sin against you. - Psalm 119:11*

The Word helps us defeat temptations. You do not have to be a victim!

Moving On

> *The law of the Lord is perfect, refreshing the soul. The statutes of the Lord are trustworthy, making wise the simple. - Psalm 19:7*

The Word revives us and brings blessings. What character trait will you grow in if you allow the Word to revive your soul?

Wisdom

What are some other passages that can help you in your Christian walk?

Romans 8; Romans 12; Ephesians and Philippians

Choose one and write it as a prayer from you to your loving Heavenly Father.

Close with a prayer of blessing on the one who came in love to share his/her journey from pain to joy. (You might even want to have refreshments and give your guest a small gift!)

WEEK 6:
OUR NEED FOR LOVE AND APPROVAL

Have you ever felt like you didn't belong? Like you were disposable?

There have been times in my life when I didn't feel like I fit. I felt like the proverbial fish out of water! I wanted God to make a way for me to disappear…but He didn't. Instead He kept telling me that He was with me and when I walked through the fire and through the flood He would be there. And, He was.

Maybe you have felt out of place or excluded or unwanted. Maybe you've experienced rejection by someone you loved and trusted. Maybe you just don't feel loved.

As we look at Bible characters we must realize that their stories are recorded for our benefit. Sometimes we will look at women in the Bible and sometimes men. The principles of the lesson will apply to you whether you are male or female.

God's Word

Read Genesis 29:15-30.

Today we are talking about a person who was unloved because of something over which she had no control. God made us in His image and we know He desires worship and that we love Him with all our heart, soul, mind and strength (Mark 12:30). We need to feel valued and loved, too. It is basic to our human nature.

What happens if that basic need is not met?

Leah was the oldest daughter of Laban but she had a physical flaw, her eyes were "weak" or "delicate". She was not a woman that men sought after. In contrast, her younger sister Rachel was stunningly beautiful and carried herself in a confidant manner. She immediately captured Jacob's heart.

But Jacob, the deceiver, was deceived. He was tricked into a marriage with Leah, a woman he did not love and did not want. But, God….

God saw Leah's broken, hurting heart. He cared and He did something. Bearing children, especially sons, was a sign of God's favor and brought great joy to a father. Leah was the first to bear a son, whom she named Reuben meaning, <u>behold a son.</u> *She said that because the Lord had seen her humiliation, now her husband would love her.*

Did he?

Then she had another son and named him Simeon, meaning <u>God hears</u> *because the Lord heard that she was unloved. Does God hear us when we feel alone and that no one cares? What are some ways He has shown you His care?*

Leah gave birth to a third son and named him Levi, meaning <u>companion</u>. She longed for a relationship with her spouse. Maybe at this point, she was willing to just be friends or companions.

Then something happened in Leah. When we are feeling so alone and unwanted we can choose to feel sorry for ourselves or to do what Leah did. At the birth of her fourth son, Leah turned her focus on the Lord. She developed her own relationship with the One who would love her completely. She worshipped God despite her circumstances. This son she named Judah, meaning <u>let Him be praised,</u> and she praised the Lord. This son would be the earthly ancestor of God's beloved Son, Jesus.

She named her fifth son Issachar, meaning <u>to hire,</u> after she bargained with her sister in order to spend the night with Jacob, and her sixth Zebulun, meaning <u>dwelling</u>, saying that the Lord had given her a gift for her husband so he would dwell with her. She also had a daughter, Dinah.

Leah could have lived a life of bitterness. Instead, she continued to love her husband even though that love was not returned. In fact, it seems that with each birth, her relationship with God grew. In the end Leah was honored by being buried with Jacob as husband and wife (Genesis 49:31)

Meeting Focus

We all need love and approval. Even if you have people who love you, you have a need for God's supernatural love. Yet, even that is a choice. Do you receive that love and live in joy and victory, knowing who you are and whose you are? Or do you live in sadness and defeat?

What are some steps we can take to walk in God's love?

Review the Victory's Journey progression. Can you identify where you are in the journey?

Next Week's Assignment

1. *Make a list of the major hurts and losses in your life from your birth to the present, and journal on times you have felt unloved, unwanted, or unwelcome. You may want to make a time line showing some good events as well as negative ones.*

2. *See Number 18 on page 155, "Additional Topics for Journaling and Sharing".*

Close with a healing prayer for all those in the group, that God will help them know how much He loves them, and that they can move in the joy of His approval.

WEEK 7:
LOSS AND GRIEF

God's Word

Loss is a part of life. If you haven't already experienced it you will. Grief is a natural healthy reaction to a loss or a painful event. It is the process of facing the pain and working through it into a stage of acceptance and renewed interest in life. It is a journey from sorrow to joy.

Every situation is unique. Grief is emotional, not intellectual, and it takes time. As we look at the grief process, remember, each grief is significant, and each person is unique in the way that they deal with their pain. As Christians, we have hope that things will get better as we put our faith in the Lord Jesus Christ.

What are some situations that produce a sense of loss?

Death, divorce (loss of family structure, security), loss of innocence or virginity, loss of trust in someone, sickness

We usually associate grief with death, but this is not the only loss we need to face. When we lose someone we love we feel loss. When someone abuses a child, they steal something from that child. It might be innocence, trust, or self-worth. Adults can be abused, too. We must allow ourselves to grieve these losses or we will be like a volcano ready to erupt either towards ourselves or others, maybe even towards God.

Read the following Scriptures about God's comfort:

Psalm 30:5, 11-12; Isaiah 61:1-3; Psalm 23; and Revelation 3:20

God is faithful and He is always there even when we are not aware of His presence. He wants to come right into the middle of our hurt and bring hope.

Meeting Focus

Grief is the process of <u>working</u> through the pain into a stage of acceptance and renewed interest in life.

It is a way to cope with extreme pain, a journey from sorrow to peace, and even joy.

This process involves several stages, but people are unique in how they work through their loss. Some people will take a step backwards to complete their journey. Others will skip a step. Because grief is emotional and not intellectual, we need to allow each person the time and understanding they need when they need it.

Jesus carried our grief on the cross. He died that we might have life and hope and healing. As Christians, we have the hope that things will get better as we put our faith

Moving On in Christ.

Grief and the grief process (An abbreviated outline is included in the workbook.):

A. *Grief is the normal, <u>healthy</u> response to loss.*

B. *The grief process is the journey of working through the pain or the loss.*

    1. *There are various stages.*

    2. *It involves <u>time</u> and <u>work.</u>*

    3. *It is unique to each individual.*

    4. *It is very emotional and often painful. Physical symptoms may be present.*

Stages of the grief process

A. *Shock*

B. *Isolation*

C. *Denial*

D. *Anger*

    1. *At deceased, others, self, God*

    2. *Blame, hostility*

E. *Fear*

    1. *Panic attacks*

    2. *Difficulty facing life, people*

F. *Guilt and severe pain – it is important that you allow yourself to feel but not to stay there. Do something healthy to release the pain.*

G. *Bargaining*

H. *Depression, anger turned inward. Friends may wonder why you aren't "better".*

    1. *Result of unrelieved anger and guilt*

    2. *Isolation and/or suicidal thoughts*

I. *Acceptance*

    1. *Understanding*

    2. *Forgiveness of person(s) who caused loss (includes deceased)*

3. Letting go of the pain, wanting to feel happy again. There may be some guilt connected to this. Remember your Heavenly Father rejoices over you; He wants you to do that too. Try short joy-trips where you do something just for fun and you choose to smile.

4. Restoration of hope in the future, normal functioning, and the ability to think of the future in a realistic way.

Helping those who are grieving

A. Approaches that hinder

    1. Lack of caring

    2. Judgmental attitudes

B. Approaches that help

    1. Awareness

    2. Listening skills

    3. Saying and doing positive things such as stopping to pray, giving a hug, being there. You may suggest they do some extra activities such as

        a. Poetry, art, writing, making a memory book or scrapbook, music

        b. Living memorials such as planting a tree, volunteering, donating Bibles through the Gideons

    4. Remind them to praise God that He is there.

Remember, the Valley of Grief is just a phase of the journey between the past and the joy God has in store for His children who ask Him for it. You matter to God! He grieves when you grieve. Isaiah 53:4 says Jesus carried our griefs. Any pain is too big for us to carry alone. Don't be stuck in a prison of pain. Let the Lord take your burden. Reach forward for your healing.

<u>Next Week's Assignment</u>

Do the following paper on "My Loss…My Feelings", then write in the journal about your losses and how you feel about each one.

Moving On

My Loss…My Feelings

Draw a picture about your loss and how you feel. Stick figures are okay.

Write God a note telling Him about your drawing:

What do you need to release to the Lord?

Write out a Scripture verse that you can hold onto as you let go of this pain:

WEEK 8:
WHAT DOES YOUR PAST LOOK LIKE?

Mike had a tough history. His father was heavily into drugs and had a major anger issue. His mother was an alcoholic. After his sister was murdered, the children were taken out of the home. In the foster system, he faced abuse and incredible loneliness. He longed to be a part of a loving family.

Mike did not want his past to define who he was or where he was headed and, yet, he kept struggling with the issues of his family. He wasn't alone!

God's Word

Joseph was a man of faith who believed in a God he did not see and in a dream that looked impossible. How do you view yourself? Do you see yourself as a failure, a big nobody, or as chosen by God with a purpose to fulfill?

Read Hebrews 11:1-3 and 22.

> *It is true that we are sinners, lacking in righteousness, and failing at godliness. As it is written: "There is no one righteous, not even one"- Romans 3:10*

BUT GOD…sent Jesus to change that. As we embrace Christ's death in our stead, accepting His love and forgiveness, we are made <u>righteous</u> *(in right standing with God). Have you accepted God's gift of forgiveness through the death and resurrection of Jesus Christ?*

As we receive Christ, God takes our human bodies and puts His Spirit into us. And He gives us purpose. We can then start living a powerful, fruitful life.

But us…too often we agree with the enemy in renouncing our value instead of renouncing his lies. Satan comes to steal…to rob…to destroy. Jesus came to bring abundant life, a life of value and fulfillment.

> *The thief comes only in order to steal and kill and destroy. I came that they may have and enjoy life, and have it in abundance (to the full, till it overflows). - John 10:10 (AMPC)*

How does the thief steal from us?

He <u>devalues</u> *us. He uses our family tree, our past, our failures to make us so lacking in power*

and in right standing with God that we just don't….

What could you possibly achieve if you really believed God had a plan and a purpose for you?

Moving On

Joseph had a history:

Noah → Shem → Nahor → Terah → Abram, Nahor, Haran, and Sarai (she had a different mother than Abram)

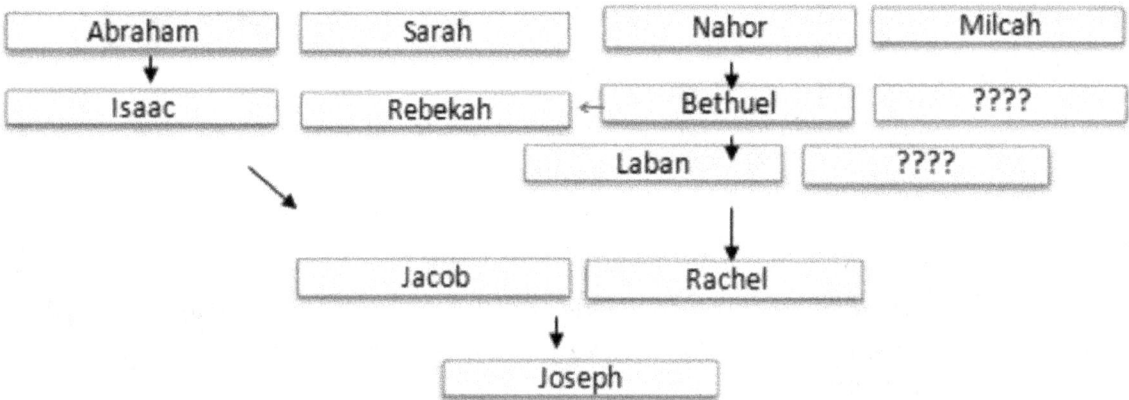

Draw a picture of your family tree:

Week 8: What Does Your Past Look Like?

Joseph's family:

On one hand Joseph had a not-so-godly heritage:

1. Noah – drunk

2. Abraham – lied about his wife

3. Sarah – impatient, abusive (with Hagar)

4. Isaac – lacked discernment

5. Rebekah – lied, favored one son, deceived her husband

6. Jacob – lied, cheated, manipulated

7. Rachel – disgraced because she was barren, jealous, stole, lied, deceived her father

On the other hand he had a godly heritage:

1. Noah – found grace in the eyes of the Lord, was used to bring salvation to humanity

2. Abraham – friend of God, man of righteousness and faith

3. Sarah – full of faith, mother of nations, fruitful in old age, beautiful, blessed

4. Isaac – godly man

5. Rebekah – beautiful, willing to follow God's plan, brave

6. Jacob – man who wrestled with God and won, his 12 sons became the 12 tribes of Israel

7. Rachel – weeping, beautiful, her barrenness turned to blessing

Joseph had a history – we all do.

He had an ancestry of imperfect people <u>who followed God.</u>

The Bible gives us true accounts of real people. It shows us where they failed but it also shows us how they followed God. The encouraging word is that regardless of the family history we carry we are chosen by God, and He has a purpose for us from the time of conception. That plan is not about our comfort or our worldly success. It is about the Kingdom. As followers of Jesus we belong to the Kingdom where He is King. In a kingdom the king is boss. In this Kingdom, Jesus is Master and Lord.

Yet it is a Kingdom where the King loves us. That is beyond human comprehension…not power control because He already has all power. Not greed because He already owns it all. Not recognition because all of creation sings His praises. He simply loves us and wants each of us to love Him back with that same unconditional love…that is the part that catches us. We get so caught up in "life" that we lose our passion and love for Jesus. Unconditional Jesus love will make us do unusual things. Unconditional love will make us pursue God's purpose for us over the "normal life".

> *The word of the Lord came to me, saying, "Before I formed you in the womb I knew you, before you were born I set you apart" - Jeremiah 1:4, 5*

We are so used to thinking we are the way we are and that is it! But Psalm 139 speaks of God having a blueprint that covers every part of His plan for our lives. In the secret place where we were formed He took great delight in drawing up our unique blueprint. He created us with the gifts and talents needed to fulfill His plan for us. He puts into our DNA the abilities and desires to accomplish the very blueprint He has for our lives.

It is God's desire to complete the work He began in us. (Phil. 1:6)

Whether or not your family history includes God followers, **you** can start your family on the faith journey.

Read Genesis 37:1-4.

> *Jacob lived in the land where his father had stayed, the land of Canaan. This is the account of Jacob's family line. Joseph, a young man of seventeen, was tending the flocks with his brothers, the sons of Bilhah and the sons of Zilpah, his father's wives, and he brought their father a bad report about them. Now Israel loved Joseph more than any of his other sons, because he had been born to him in his old age; and he made an ornate robe for him. When his brothers saw that their father loved him more than any of them, they hated him and could not speak a kind word to him.*

The robe was a symbol of possible transfer of authority. Was this a wise move on Jacob's part? Why, or why not?

Do parents sometimes set kids up?

Then Joseph had several dreams (Genesis 37:5-11). He told his brothers, and then his father. What were their reactions (verses 8 and 11)?

They hated him and could not even speak to him in a civil tone. Jacob pondered it in his heart.

Meeting Focus

How can we tell the difference between a God-given dream or vision and something from our own imagination or mindset?

It will match up with the teaching of God's Word, and there will be a sense in our spirit that this is God's will. We will have peace about it. Circumstances will open doors when it is God's time, and others may confirm it.

Week 8: What Does Your Past Look Like?

God knows your destiny and He wants you to know it so you can take steps in the right direction. Faith believes a promise it doesn't see. Do you dare to believe?

God is not as concerned about your past heritage as you are. The Bible is filled with stories of people who did great things for God. Many of them had troubled pasts. It is to the glory of God when we grow and fulfill God's purpose for us despite our family heritage or our own personal past. God is about what you are doing now to prepare for your eternal inheritance.

Don't miss out by holding back, but go forward and become victorious!

Next Week's Assignment

1. *Journal on past family or personal background situations that hold you back from being all you could be. You could continue to do your own family tree.*

2. *Fill in the paper, "Inventory of Sins and Weaknesses". Ask God to speak to your heart. Then read Ephesians, chapters 4-6.*

3. *Explain the page, "Inventory of Sins and Weaknesses". Define current, past, and generational issues:*

    Current – those you are dealing with now

    Past – before today.

    Generational – repeated tendencies or behaviors in your family line

Moving On

Inventory of Sins and Weaknesses

(Mark current issues, past issues, and generational issues. Be honest.)

Sin/Weakness	Current	Past	Generational
Pride			
Rebellion			
Self-pity			
Worldly values			
Bitterness			
Malice or evil speaking			
Disregard for God's rules (such as keeping the Sabbath, honoring those in authority, having no other "gods")			
Ingratitude			
Lying			
Pornography			
Stealing			
Devil worship			
Laziness			
Procrastination			
Immoral thoughts and/or actions (lust)			
Addictions			
Envy/jealousy			
Fear			
Depression & despair (with or without suicidal thoughts)			
Negative thinking			
Hypocrisy			
Anxiety or worry			

Write a prayer confessing the sins and weaknesses you marked. Renounce the effect they have had on you and your family. Ask Jesus to make you clean.

WEEK 9:
SECRETS TO DEFEATING SINS

Meeting Focus

Helen could not speak English when she started school. It was a big school with crowded conditions. Because of her language deficit, her teachers decided she was not smart enough to be in a regular classroom so they moved her to a classroom of children with mental and social disabilities. They told her parents that she could not understand the basic things of life. That is why when the only doll she ever had was taken away and given to her sister, her family thought it was okay.

This little girl grew up thinking she was unable to function. When she seemed normal her mother explained that her mental illness would show itself when she reached puberty. She married and had children, and all the time, she waited. She just knew one day she would wake up, and her life would fall apart...

Until she went through the "Victory's Journey" program and realized she was smart and pretty and fully functional! It was a life-changer. She could rewrite the rest of her life!

Think about how you see yourself. Was this always the way you felt?

Much of how we act is based on who we think we are. If someone told you you will never be smart enough to do a certain thing you will probably act like you are not smart enough.

People often continue this negativity by the type of self-talking they engage in. It is our choice if we believe the truth or lies. It is also our choice what we say to ourselves and how we present ourselves.

Talk about ways that people deal with painful issues, using the "Progression of Healing" in the workbook on page 14. Sometimes the ways that we learn to deal with hurts as children are the ways we deal with them as adults. Also, the way you view yourself as a child will be good unless you have been hurt. (Most people have!) After a hurt we change our self-view. With God's help we can face our past and alter the way we see ourselves and the way we react to conform to the truth of the Bible. It is always better to do and see things God's way!

Look at the "Inventory of Sins and Weaknesses" that you filled out. What did you learn by doing this paper? Did you notice any familial trends?

Do you have some negative feelings about yourself? What are they?

Can you pinpoint when you started feeling that way? What words or situation might have started

Moving On

that self-view? It would be a good idea to do some journaling about this.

God's Word

Negative feelings definitely influence how we behave, but sometimes we have sin that we need to confront and deal with. We need God's help to have a victorious life.

Sexual sin should also be discussed. How deeply you go into this depends on the group. God is explicit about this in His Word. However, He also offers freedom in this area, regardless of our past offense. When a sexual union takes place, a spiritual, emotional, and physical bond is established as well. But God has given us a way to break those bonds and be restored to Him as virgins – just as if we had never sinned!

As a group, look at the biblical view of sexual immorality and fornication:

> *You shall not commit adultery. - Exodus 20:14*

> *Do you not know that your bodies are members of Christ himself? Shall I then take the members of Christ and unite them with a prostitute? Never! Do you not know that he who unites himself with a prostitute is one with her in body? For it is said, "The two will become one flesh". But he who unites himself with the Lord is one with him in spirit. Flee from sexual immorality. All other sins a man commits are outside the body, but he who sins sexually sins against their own body. Do you not know that your bodies are temples of the Holy Spirit, who is in you, whom you have received from God? You are not your own; you were bought at a price. Therefore honor God with your bodies.- 1 Corinthians 6:15-20*

Ask participants for their definition of sexual sin/fornication.

The Bible uses the Greek word "porneia". It is most often translated as "fornication" and is used in at least five ways:

1. Voluntary sexual intercourse of an unmarried person with someone of the opposite sex. (1 Cor. 7:2; 1 Thess, 4:3)

2. A synonym for adultery (Matt. 5:27-28)

3. Harlotry and prostitution (Rev. 2:14, 20)

4. Homosexuality and lesbianism (Gen. 19:4-7; 1 Cor. 6:9; 1 Tim. 1:10)

5. Sexual intercourse with close relatives (Leviticus 18)

It can also include pornography. Pornography involves visualizing and imagining sexual sin. Notice the Greek root word.

The Bible gives us examples of people who fall prey to sexual sin. Although God condemns the sin He forgives and restores the sinner who repents. That is God's part. There is NO ONE God cannot redeem!

Week 9: Secrets To Defeating Sin

1. David (2 Sam 11-12; Psalm 51)
2. Woman at the well (John 4:6-42)
3. Woman with alabaster box (Luke 7:36-50)
4. Woman caught in adultery (John 8:1-11)

Our part is to pray a prayer asking God to help us return to sexual purity and mean it. Then we need to live it out by choosing what we will focus our thoughts on and by submitting to God. Accountability helps!

As you teach this lesson stress the importance of God's Word in victorious living.

To defeat sin and overcome evil, we must put on the armor of God and use the powerful offensive weapon mentioned in Ephesians 6. What is that?

It is the Sword of the Spirit which is the Word of God.

Why do you think God's Word is called the Sword of the Spirit? Read Hebrews 4:12.

> *For the word of God is living and active. Sharper than any double-edged sword, it penetrates even to dividing soul and spirit, joints and marrow; it judges the thoughts and attitudes of the heart. -Hebrews 4:12*

How can we use God's Word on our own thinking patterns?

- Read the Bible. Ponder what you read. Memorize key verses.
- Journal on what God is saying to you through the verse(s) you read.
- Map out a plan for applying the principles you are learning.
- Be accountable.

Paul writes that we should have the mind of <u>Christ</u> in Philippians 2:5. That is our goal. We need to replace wrong thinking and behavior with godly thinking and behavior. It is not enough to renounce personal and generational sin. We must fill our hearts with Jesus. As Paul wrote to the Christians in the Ephesian church, the Holy Spirit is also talking to us.

Read and write Ephesians 4:21-24 as a prayer.

We can take every thought we have and make it obedient to Christ.

> *For though we live in the world, we do not wage war as the world does.*
> *The weapons we fight with are not the weapons of the world. On the contrary, they have divine power to demolish strongholds. We demolish arguments and every pretension that sets itself up against the knowledge of God, and we take captive every thought to make it obedient to Christ. - 2 Corinthians 10:3-5*

Moving On

Notice the use of the word, "we". Circle it every time it is used in this passage. We must put out the effort, using the weapons we have been given – the Word, prayer, praise, support from other brothers and sisters - always relying on the Holy Spirit.

Teach the following lesson with careful focus on each point:

Steps to Defeating Sin

1. *Identify problem areas*

> A. *Generational issues – passed down family weaknesses, attitudes and behaviors such as depression, anger, martyr attitudes, insecurity, fear, bitterness, pride, lust, abuse, control, etc. – Exodus 20:3-6*
>
> B. *Blind spots – problems you have but do not see in yourself. It may be the very thing that really bothers you about someone else. Denying a problem prevents God from making you everything He wants you to be.*
>
>> *1. Ask a spouse or close friend to help you see areas you are blind to.*
>>
>> *2. Observe the way people respond to you at different times.*
>>
>> *3. Ask yourself if your actions bring glory to God.*
>>
>> *4. Identify your motives when you feel upset.*
>
> C. *Strongholds – areas of frequent temptations that are so strong they result in feelings of failure, hopelessness, defeat. Victories do not last. These may be generational or may be the result of giving Satan a foothold.*
>
>> *1. Were you honest on your personal inventory paper?*
>>
>> *2. Look up each item you checked in your concordance and read ALL the verses listed. It may take a while! Get God's perspective on the sin and allow that to change your perspective.*

2. *Referring to your inventory of sins and weaknesses, fill out the grid "Defeating Sin's Power In My Life"*

> A. *Confess these carnal weaknesses, strongholds, and blind spots as sins that God hates.*
>
> B. *Renounce the sins that have hindered you.*
>
> C. *Ask Jesus to forgive you and cleanse you from these sins.*
>
> D. *Thank Jesus that you are clean. When Satan tries to trip you, remind him of the blood of Jesus that covers you. Quote a Scripture at him such as 1 John 1:9.*

Week 9: Secrets To Defeating Sin

E. Have a specific goal, prayer, and Scripture for each area.

F. Walk in the light, refusing to allow your mind to go back to even consider the old thoughts.

G. Fill the empty places with good Christ-like attitudes and actions. Do good for others whether you feel like it or not. Pray for those who have hurt you.

Defeating Sin's Power in My Life

Sin(s) to put off	Christlike traits to put on	Prayer	Scripture(s)

Put off the old attitudes and actions and put on the new man (attitudes and actions of Jesus) according to Ephesians 4:22-27, 29-32:

... put off your old self, which is being corrupted by its deceitful desires; to be made new in the attitude of your minds; and to put on the new self, created to be like God in true righteousness and holiness.

Therefore each of you must put off falsehood and speak truthfully to his neighbor, for we are all members of one body. "In your anger do not sin": Do not let the sun go down while you are still angry, and do not give the devil a foothold.

Do not let any unwholesome talk come out of your mouths, but only what is helpful for

building others up according to their needs, that it may benefit those who listen.
And do not grieve the Holy Spirit of God, with whom you were sealed for the day of redemption. Get rid of all bitterness, rage and anger, brawling and slander, along with every form of malice. Be kind and compassionate to one another, forgiving each other, just as in Christ God forgave you.

Notice all the behaviors mentioned in Ephesians. This is a great little guide for acting like Jesus.

Give no place to the devil.

Also read Ephesians 5:1-21 and Colossians 3:1-15. Notice that we do the "putting off" and "putting on". It is our responsibility to actively start working towards our goal.

Pray with each person who wishes to renounce a sin or generational problem. As they renounce it agree with them, then pray that God will help them to walk in His freedom.

3. Believe that God is on your side. You have renounced your sins. You have asked His forgiveness. You are chosen by God to be His own beloved child. You are pure! Read Ephesians 1:3-8.

4. Commit yourself to living a life of service to Jesus Christ, that He might be honored in every thought, word, and action.

5. Expect His guidance and leading as He takes you into new dimensions of personal worship and service. Step out in faith, a little at a time. Don't let fear or past failures determine your future!

6. Expect His favor on your efforts to please Him. (But be sensitive to His leading through others.)

7. Pray the prayer of Jabez in 1 Chronicles 4:10 daily:

Jabez cried out to the God of Israel, "Oh, that you would bless me and enlarge my territory! Let your hand be with me, and keep me from harm so that I will be free from pain." And God granted his request.

Next Week's Assignment

1. Fill in the chart on "Defeating Sin's Power in my Life" with a personal prayer and a Scripture for each sin. It is good to memorize these Scriptures or write them on a paper to keep handy. That way they can be quoted to the enemy when he tries to tempt or discourage you.

2. (Optional) If someone in the group has sexual sin in his/her past, journaling is important. A letter of forgiveness to oneself can open a door of healing.

3. Ask God to reveal any bondages that still need to be broken. Have each one renounce

Week 9: Secrets To Defeating Sin

these and thank God for His forgiveness and restoration to purity.

4. Fill out the paper "From Child to Adult" and journal on how you respond.

5. Read the book of Philippians. Then reread Chapter One, writing down some key thoughts and impressions. What you write down may minister to someone else.

6. Make Psalm 139:23 your daily prayer this week.

Pray Psalm 139:23 as a group.

Search me, O God, and know my heart; test me and know my anxious thoughts.

Moving On

From Child to Adult

A. Put checks by the reactions you had as a child. Double check the reactions you still have.

1. Blamed self (guilt feelings)
2. Blamed others - maybe even God
3. Feelings of never "being good enough"
4. Need to hurt or punish self
5. Need to hurt or punish others
6. Denial
7. Acted as a follower without responsibility
8. Physical "sickness"
9. Tried to do better
10. Tried to be strong, the "adult"

B. Check the traits you think are important. Initial the traits you have now.

1. Independence
2. Creativity
3. Loyalty
4. Perseverance
5. Kindness
6. Honesty
7. Poise and confidence
8. Problem solving skills
9. Patience
10. Faith

C. List two negative reactions you wish to change:

D. List two positives you have that you wish to grow in:

Now, choose a single area and ask God to help you change. Look up 3 verses that show how God can help you in that area. Read 1 Corinthians 13:11. Journal on how you will do that.

WEEK 10:
OUR CONFIDENCE

Open with prayer and ask if anyone would like to share a testimony since joining Victory's Journey. Review the Motto and Group Guidelines.

God's Word

We will be starting a five-week study of the letter to the Philippians as it applies to our group and the journey we are on. Each group has its unique needs and ministry opportunities. You may occasionally need to spend more time on a certain verse than you'd expected. It is not necessary to always complete the plan for that week. Just pick up where you stopped next week.

Do you trust God? Think about it. Trust may come easily for you if promises that were made to you were kept but, for many, that isn't the case. Hannah was told that if she was really good she would get to have a friend over for a sleepover and so she was! In fact, she did extra chores and worked as hard as a ten year old ever could. But the promise was not kept. That happened again and again. Hannah stopped expecting good results. Her heart grew hard, her grades plummeted and so did every other aspect of her life.

Disappointments lead to disillusionment and disillusionment leads to utter defeat. Why try to be good if it doesn't make a difference? Why even care?!

People may fail us...and they often do. Those hurts leave scars and we become very skilled at turning off real feelings. Being vulnerable is out of the question!

But the Bible teaches us that God is good (Psalm 100:5). Good people act good. They do good things. Therefore, if God is good we can believe He acts good. He wants to bless us and do what is good for us. How much do you think God has for you if you will dare to be vulnerable and let Him into the scarred places?

When Paul wrote this letter, or epistle, he was being treated unfairly. Grace and peace do not come naturally or easily when we are being wronged. Yet, we see they were the real results of his being in the presence of Christ.

As you go through the Bible passages, encourage the group to give their observations first. Then add your thoughts.

Discuss the following verses from Philippians 1:

In verse 2, who gives us grace and peace?

God our Father and the Lord Jesus Christ

Moving On

Is it difficult to think of God giving good gifts?

We have looked at what God's Word says about God as our Parent. Are you starting to see a difference in the way you view Him now?

Ask if they are still comparing Him to a parent?

Read 2 Corinthians 1:3. How does this verse describe God?

The Father of Compassion and the God of all Comfort

In verses 3-5, how did Paul pray for the believers at Philippi?

With joy

Joy is not dependent on our circumstances for as we read through this letter we learn that Paul is writing from a jail cell.

Verse 6 is the key verse for the "Victory's Journey" program. What does it say to you?

Isn't it good to know that Jesus, your Good Shepherd, wants a complete healing in your life, and He will patiently do what is necessary to accomplish it.

Rewrite this verse as a prayer of thanksgiving to your Loving Heavenly Father.

What feelings do you pick up from Paul in verses 7-8?

He carries them in his heart and it feels right to do so. He longs for them.

Read verse 9. List the three key ingredients of a successful group?

1. <u>Love</u>

2. <u>Knowledge</u>

3. <u>Deep insight</u>

Love, knowledge, and depth of insight help us bond and trust one another. The more we know others the more we can love and trust them...that's true of God, too.

In verse 11 of Philippians one, who is the Source of righteousness?

Jesus Christ

Does this mean we will have an easy life as we live for Jesus? Look at verses 12 to 26. Note Paul's attitude in various difficult situations.

God's purpose is greater than ours. What seemed to be a negative in Paul's life helped others open up and share their faith more freely. We can be that person who helps someone else just by being open.

Week 10: Our Confidence

God's plans for you are good. He asks us to be good and to act in a good way. Other people's actions do not need to determine our behavior. We are responsible for what we do now.

Notice some of the admonitions Paul gives these Christians in verses 27 to 30. Pick one that applies to you.

Encourage your group members to share. It is healthy to set goals as we mature in our Christian walk. Goals are only good though, if they involve action. What actions are they willing to do to grow in these areas?

How has the chart from last week on Defeating Sin's Power helped them? Ask each person to share one item and the verse God showed them.

Review the paper, "From Child to Adult". How did you feel as you wrote in your journal? Share something you wrote with your group or with someone you trust.

It is important that we face our issues so we can grow in the knowledge of God's love and grace. Once we face them we can recognize what we are doing and take steps to change our patterns.

Meeting Focus

Review "From Child to Adult". Ask how each one felt as they wrote in their journal. Ask them to share something they wrote or a pleasant memory.

Next Week's Assignment

1. Draw a picture of your family.

2. Memorize a verse that speaks to you from "My Value in Christ", and then write in your journal about it. Answer the question, "How does that make me feel?"

3. Reread Philippians 2:1-13 and answer the questions in the workbook.

My Value in Christ

In Matthew I am
- 5:14 - light to the world

In John I am
- 1:12 - God's child
- 15:15 - Christ's friend
- 15:16 - chosen to bear fruit

In Romans I am
- 6:18 - a slave of righteousness
- 8:14-17 – a child of God and a joint heir with Christ

In 1 Corinthians I am
- 3:16; 6:19 – a dwelling place for the Spirit of God
- 12:27 – a member of Christ's Body

In 2 Corinthians I am
- 5:17 - a new creation
- 5:18, 19 – reconciled to God and able to pass that on

In Ephesians I am
- 1:1 – a saint
- 2:10 – God's workmanship
- 2:6, 19 – a citizen of God's Kingdom
- 4:24 - righteous and holy

In Colossians I am
- 3:3 – hidden in Christ
- 3:12 – chosen, holy, and dearly loved

In 1 Peter I am
- 2:9, 10 – chosen, part of God's royal priesthood, God's own possession

In 1 John I am
- 3:1, 2 – a child of God who will resemble Christ when He comes for His Church
- 5:18 – born of God and the evil one (Satan) cannot touch me

WEEK 11:
WHO AM I?

Open by singing a chorus along with a CD and having prayer.

God's Word

Discuss Philippians 2:1-13:

In Philippians 2:1 we have a great encouragement in being one with Christ. Take time to consider the wonderful position that places us in as Christians. It is easier to deal with past hurts when one knows one is in a positive meaningful relationship with the King of Kings.

Love provides comfort. You are loved! Allow yourself to feel Christ's love and comfort. His love took Him to Gethsemane and Calvary. Think about His rejection, His death, His shame, His grief, and that He did it for you so you would not have to carry those burdens. There is fellowship with the Holy Spirit, the third Person of the Trinity, Who walks alongside the believer. We are not alone anymore.

In verses 2-4 we see that the life of love and service requires us to be one in <u>spirit and purpose.</u>

What characteristics should we adopt and what things should we avoid if we are to be like Christ?

In verses 5-11, note the attitude of Christ. Do an attitude check. What were the positive effects of Christ's attitude in verses 9 through 11?

What positive attitudes are you working on?

Verses 12-13 tell us that God has a purpose. We need to let Him lead us to its completion.

Hebrews 12:1-2 tells us to cast off our weights. Then healing can be expected.

What regrets do you have?

What stresses you? What fears or insecurities hold you back from being totally free in Christ?

What weights do you need to cast into the ocean of God's love?

Journal on the weights you need to release to Jesus.

Meeting Focus

Review the paper, "My Value in Christ". Name and discuss some principles of truth that we must accept and hold on to, such as the fact that we are forgiven through Jesus Christ. We must each choose what we will believe, the Bible or Satan's lies. Valuing yourself means thanking God for making you and then caring for yourself. We are children of worth.

Talk about the Workbook pages on "Regret or Self-Control" and "Dealing with Guilt".

Moving On

Next Week's Assignment

1. Write in your journal about a fear or insecurity and do the papers on "Regret or Self Contempt" and "Dealing with Guilt".

2. Read Philippians 2:14-30 and journal on positive and negative relationships you are in now. How do you think your childhood relationships set the patterns for these relationships?

"Dealing with Guilt" is based on David's prayer to the Lord after his sin. His cry is one of desperation but also one of faith in who God is. God so loved us that He gave us His one and only Son. His love is a forever love.

It doesn't stop. But sometimes we fail Him. That is when we need to repent and seek His face.

Remember what He says to us in 1 John 1:9:

> But if we confess our sins to him, he is faithful and just to forgive us our sins and to cleanse us from all wickedness. (NLT)

Week 11: Who Am I?

Regret or Self-Contempt

God's Forgiveness

If we confess our sins, he is faithful and just and will forgive us our sins and purify us from all unrighteousness. - 1 John 1:9

After God's Forgiveness

Regret - accepting that forgiveness but wishing it had not happened, knowing it cannot be undone, awareness of broken pieces of life, confidence that God uses broken pieces to make something beautiful…

or

Self-contempt – feeling that "I have failed in a certain area" means "I am a failure" and "I will always be a failure", the inability to move beyond self-hate, the inability to see newness in Christ, choosing to receive Satan's accusations as truth.

How I View Myself	How God Wants Me to View Myself

Thought Questions:

1. What is the truth?

2. What will I choose to do with this truth?

3. What is my future hope based on this truth?

Moving On

Dealing with Guilt

Unfounded guilt is blame the enemy or other people put on you, often for things they have done. Stepping into freedom only happens when we can identify our feelings of guilt and then decide if they are false guilt feelings or real guilt feelings. If they are false guilt feelings we must give them to Christ and refuse to take them back. This takes choosing to speak only truth to ourselves.

Name any guilt feelings you have and decide if they are false or true.

True guilt is something that God will forgive you of if you ask Him. Read Psalm 51 and answer the following questions:

1. What are your sins? (verse 3)

2. Who do we really sin against when we sin? (verse 4)

3. What does the psalmist rely on when he asks for forgiveness? (verses 1,6,14)

4. What sacrifice pleases God? (verse 17)

5. What hope can we have? (verses 7-12)

6. What is our responsibility after we are forgiven and restored? (verses 13-15)

Other Scriptures to read are as follows: Ezra 9:5-7, Nehemiah 1:5-7, Psalm 32:5, Psalm 38:4-18, Acts 19:18, Hebrews 10:19-22, James 5:16, and 1 John 1:9. (Write out one of these Scriptures that ministered to you.)

Journal: Write a prayer of thanksgiving to God for removing your guilt. If He has removed it what right do you have to bring it back up? Memorize your prayer and use it against the enemy when he tries to remind you of your past.

WEEK 12:
TRUTH OR LIES?

God's Word

Discuss Philippians 2:14-30:

Focus on relationships, positive and negative.

How did Paul want them to behave? (Without complaining or arguing so they would become blameless and pure and shine in a dark world.)

Why? (See verses 14-17, 19, and 27-28.)

What other Scriptures deal with our relationships?

You can choose to discuss the following passages:

Psalm 27:17; 2 Timothy 1:16; John 15:15; 1 Peter 3:8; Joshua 1:5; John 17:21

Meeting Focus

What do you believe is true about yourself?

Talk about our identity in Christ and how we need to act as the people we really are. This is a great opening to get to know how each person views himself/herself and to address problems from the past. Discuss the papers "Regret or Self-Contempt" and "Dealing With Guilt".

What is a godly self-view?

Review the Group Guidelines briefly and comment on how they serve to help develop healthy relationships within the group and, ultimately, in all areas of life. Let each person share something that they wrote in their journals.

Explain the papers, "Response to Anger" and "Anger's Actions".

Read Mark 4:35-41:

> *That day when evening came, he said to his disciples, "Let us go over to the other side."*
>
> *Leaving the crowd behind, they took him along, just as he was, in the boat. There were also other boats with him. A furious squall came up, and the waves broke over the boat, so that it was nearly swamped. Jesus was in the stern, sleeping on a cushion. The disciples woke him and said to him, "Teacher, <u>don't you care</u> if we drown?"*
>
> *He got up, rebuked the wind and said to the waves, "Quiet! Be still!" Then the wind died down and it was completely calm.*

Moving On

> *He said to his disciples, "Why are you so afraid? Do you still have no faith?"*
>
> *They were terrified and asked each other, "Who is this? Even the wind and the waves obey him!"*

Did Jesus care?

Yes! He may have been testing their faith. That is something we all struggle with when the storms of life swirl around us.

Why were they terrified after the wind died down and the seas were calm?

They saw the supernatural up close and very personal! In answer to their questioning if Jesus cared, He did something they knew was impossible. He also proved that they mattered to Him. You matter to Him!

> *And we know that in all things God works for the good of those who love him, who have been called according to his purpose. For those God foreknew he also predestined to be conformed to the likeness of his Son, that he might be the firstborn among many brothers and sisters. -Romans 8:28 & 29*

Ask, *"How do these verses make you feel?"*

God is good!!!

Next Week's Assignment

1. Read Philippians 3 and journal.

2. Do the papers "Response To Anger" and "Anger's Actions".

3. Journal on a good result that came from one of your past pains.

Ask God to bless them with faith that He is the One in their boat of pain and when He says "Be still!" the storm must obey. Pray for courage and for healing.

Week 12: Truth Or Lies

Response to Anger

1. What triggers my anger?

2. Do I always react the same way when I am angry or when I feel one of my "rights" is threatened?

3. Is my perception of the situation true? Do I know all the facts? Do I know both sides?

4. Have I asked God to let me know the truth?

5. Could there be a different way of looking at this?

6. Am I at fault?

7. Have I prayed for the other person(s) involved?

8. Do I feel God's love towards the other person(s) involved? Can I accept this person as he (or she) is and as loved by my loving heavenly Father?

9. Do I love him (or her) and God enough to do what it takes to heal the division? (ie. Ask forgiveness for my part?)

10. Am I willing to release my feelings and "rights" to the Lord and let them go?

11. Is my heart's prayer, "Lord, change me"?

    A. Make me more humble like Jesus in Phil. 2.

    B. Develop certain character qualities (or fruit) or spiritual gifts in me.

    C. Correct me and change my ways through God's loving discipline.

    D. Prepare me for greater responsibility or leadership.

12. Do I believe the Holy Spirit will help me?

    And we know that in all things God works for the good of those who love him, who have been called according to his purpose. For those God foreknew he also predestined to be conformed to the image of his Son, that he might be the firstborn among many brothers. - Roman 8:28 & 29

Moving On

Anger's Actions

Briefly describe a time when you felt angry (or frustrated or irritated) this past week:

Check the way you express your anger:

__loud voice	__harsh words	__slander
__drugs or alcohol	__foolish behavior	__malice (meanness)
__glaring eyes	__wrong dress	__strife, division
__verbal abuse	__avoidance	__profanity
__stealing	__vandalism	__rape
__pornography	__clenched teeth	__lying
__worry	__blaming	__depression
__abuse	__arguing	__fretting
__irritability	__lack of appreciation	__fear
__door slamming	__over-sleeping	__lack of patience
__silent treatment	__denial	__abnormal eating

Who is usually the target of your anger?

When did you start using these "anger actions"?

Pick a verse in Psalm 31 to use as a prayer and pray it each night and morning to the Lord

WEEK 13:
FREEDOM FROM ANGER

Nurture the developing bonds by listening to a song on tape.

God's Word

Discuss Philippians 3:

Have you ever felt that your faith had become a little frayed? When we are struggling with difficult issues we can easily lose our focus on the Lord.

Read Philippians 3:1. What is a key that Paul gives us to guard our faith?

Rejoicing and reading his letter. For us, worship and the Word.

James tells us that faith without works is dead (James 2:17). Works are good but they do not get us into God's Kingdom. In Philippians 3:2-7, what attitude should we have towards relying on our good works for God's grace?

We should consider all our human successes as loss.

Sometimes we also hold on to hurts and fears. How does holding on to such things make us feel?

Is it hard to give up our attitudes towards our past achievements or our past mistreatments?

Verses 8-11 are a powerful statement of what is important in our relationship with Jesus Christ. What is our goal?

Resurrection from the dead. That is our hope as we know Christ and walk in His righteousness through faith in Him.

Why does God allow certain things to happen?

People make choices. Our free will allows us to do that. Is God responsible when we make bad choices? Or when others choose to hurt us?

Discuss choices people make. God has given us the right to choose to serve Him. (See Joshua 24:14-15.)

Consider Christ's righteousness. How do individuals achieve righteousness?

By faith.

Moving On

What purposes might God have in allowing people to suffer pain?

He wants us to mature in Christ, be a witness to others, and draw closer to Jesus.

What purposes might He have in your situation?

He is preparing you to be able to accomplish the purpose He has prepared for your life.

Look at Matthew, chapters 23-25.

As Paul talks about striving towards knowing Jesus and being able to share in the resurrection from the dead, he stresses the value of faith. Suffering may be a part of our lives. Maybe you have suffered and you don't understand why. Read verses 1, 8, and 10 again. Summarize what they tell us.

Rejoice! And consider knowing Jesus more important than anything else.

Read Philippians 3: 12-16.

The past may be filled with good things or difficult things. We must look at the past, deal with it, and then be willing to put it behind us before we can truly move forward into God's plan for us.

Review Philippians 1:6.

God is at work in us making us complete in Christ.

Our goal is to win the prize of eternal life. How are we to strive towards that goal?

In Philippians 3:17 to 4:1 Paul tells the Philippians to imitate him and others who follow him.

How can you do that?

Is Jesus able to transform hurt individuals? What is our part in the first verse of chapter 4?

To stand firm!

Meeting Focus

Ask the group what they learned from doing the two papers on anger.

As we consider our past and the choices we have about how we will deal with it, we need to take a look at anger. Anger is just an emotion but if not handled properly, it will be destructive to others and to us.

Week 13: Freedom From Anger

Anger occurs when we feel that our rights have been violated. Little children often "stuff" their anger to cope with the pain. That is not healthy.

Teach the following lesson:

Steps To Freedom From Anger

Moses was God's man, but when he saw an Egyptian beating an Israelite he reacted. His emotions took over, and he killed the Egyptian. As a result of his anger he was forced to leave all he knew and flee to a distant desert.

Anger in itself is just an <u>emotion</u> or feeling, neither good nor bad. It is what we do with it that can destroy us and others. That is sin and sin produces bondage. The more we give in to any bondage the more powerful it becomes. Angry people will say hurtful things, try to control the lives of others, be verbally and physically abusive, act impulsively, and cause tension in their environments. Unchecked anger often prevents people from living effective Christian lives. Attempting to control the anger leads to more and more stress.

Anger takes two primary forms: overt hostility towards others or passive anger turned inward, known as depression. Both forms steal life and joy. God's Word holds the key to victorious living!

Those who have been hurt usually have some feelings of anger. If a person has had at least five of the following symptoms in the same two-week period, and one of these is a loss of interest or a depressed mood, he/she is probably suffering from depression:

- A depressed or irritable mood most of the day
- Lessened interest or pleasure in daily activities
- Significant weight loss or gain when not dieting
- Insomnia or hypersomnia
- Agitated or slowed behavior, fatigue
- Feelings of worthlessness or guilt that are inappropriate
- Inability to concentrate
- Recurrent thoughts of dying
- Isolation

In such a situation it is a good idea to suggest that they speak with their doctor.

It is important that you understand the difference between depression and normal grief. It is normal to grieve over losses. Refer to the lesson on "Grief and the Grief Process".

Moving On

If someone is overtly hostile deal with that situation immediately. Remain calm. While the co-leader may need to call for help in an extreme situation, most of the time a group crisis is resolved as the person is allowed to vent in a safe, calm atmosphere. Of course, all members of the group need to be and feel safe during any such confrontation. If the person is acting out toward one of the leaders the other leader needs to be the one dealing directly with them.

The key to freedom from anger is to want to change. These are vital steps in helping you find that freedom:

1. *Identify the <u>cause</u>.*
2. *Get the <u>facts</u>!*
3. *Accept personal <u>responsibility</u>. (Ephesians 4:31, 32; Colossians 3:8)*
4. *See your anger through the <u>eyes</u> of those you are hurting.*
5. *Use your anger as an <u>opportunity</u> to deal with the real issue.*
6. *Act <u>quickly</u> to recall and correct past offenses.*
7. *Regain <u>surrendered</u> areas from the enemy (Satan) —see Ephesians 6:12.*
    a. *Confess the sin that caused the anger.*
    b. *Claim the power of the blood of Jesus.*
    c. *Ask God to take back any area(s) in which you have allowed Satan to get a stronghold.*
    d. *Submit that area of your life 100% to God.*
    e. *Memorize and quote Scripture when the enemy attacks you.*
8. *Forgive your <u>offenders</u> – be willing to carry their pain —see Matthew 18:21-35.*
9. *Find the <u>benefits</u> from the events that caused you to react.*
10. *Give God all your <u>personal rights</u>.*
11. *Be <u>accountable</u>.*
12. *Be <u>filled</u> with the Holy Spirit.*

   Be angry and do not sin; ponder in your own heart and be silent. Selah (Pause and think about that.) -Psalm 4:4 (ESV)

Next Week's Assignment

1. Read Philippians 4. Write how verse 3 applies to your group.

2. Begin to memorize a meaningful verse from Philippians 4 or "My Value in Christ".

3. Write in your journal why you chose the above verse and what you need God to help you with.

Close in prayer. Have the group members pray for one another.

WEEK 14:
CARING FOR ONE ANOTHER

God's Word

Ask each one to quote the verse that they memorized this past week. It doesn't have to be perfect.

Discuss Philippians 4:

(Always encourage the group members to share their insights first.)

God created Adam, and He said, "It is not good for man to be alone." That is the only time during creation that God said something was not good. We humans are different from animals in that we are created in the likeness of God Himself and deep within us there is a void that cries for relationship. We need a relationship with God to have abundant life, but we also need relationships with other humans. Yet sometimes good relationships turn sour.

Can you think of some reasons good friendships fall apart?

Different interests, jealousy, hurtful words, lack of caring about the other person

In Philippians 4:2-3 we read about two godly women who loved the Lord and worked hard in ministry. We don't know what the disagreement was about, but it was big enough for Paul to address it. Conflict affects the whole body and can be very hurtful.

What does Paul ask these Christian women to do?

To agree with each other in the Lord.

What does he ask the church leader to do?

Help them.

Notice the lack of harshness. Helping each other work through issues is part of the benefits of being part of a body of believers.

How does helping one another apply to those in "*Victory's Journey*"?

The small group dynamics are geared to our being there for each other. We are a team moving together towards the prize. Each person is important to everyone in the group. One person's encouragement or smile may help someone else make it!

Read Philippians 4:4-9.

Compare verse 4 to Philippians 3:1, Ephesians 5:19, 20 and Psalm 50:23 (NIV). Why is this principle of rejoicing so important?

Moving On

It takes our focus off of us and puts it on Jesus, where it belongs.

Philippians 4:6-9 lists some truths that can help us deal with fears and panic attacks. What is our role in attaining peace of mind?

We need to surround our thoughts and prayers with thanksgiving. Keeping our focus on good things is a guard against Satan's darts.

In verse 10, what are some practical ways we can care for others?

Let your concern become action.

In Philippians 4:11-18, what secret has Paul learned?

He had learned contentment regardless of his situation.

What does the word "contentment" mean to you? Is your spirit at rest?

In verse 13, we can see that this ability to be content in every situation is related to Paul's relationship with Christ, the Source of all strength.

The Philippians had served God well by ministering to Paul's needs whenever they had a chance. Because of their compassion put into <u>action</u>, Paul was blessed and able to continue in ministry.

What do our gifts become when we help those who serve God?

They are a fragrant offering, an acceptable sacrifice. They are credited to our account. We actually have a share in the ministry!

What gifts do you have that God might need you to share with someone in need?

Be prepared to encourage each member of the group in something you see in them that God can use. This could be a positive journaling assignment in which they remember childhood dreams and things they enjoyed doing.

Verses 19-23 of this chapter close the letter with praise, encouragement and victory! All your needs means all your needs. Christ is and has all we need! We are to live every part of our lives for His glory and it is His grace in our spirits that enables us to be victorious!

Meeting Focus

Have a time of sharing the principles in Philippians 4. Encourage each one to share something they have written (or thought) about this past week. Even if it is something small, it is important that all share. If one of them has a particularly hard time sharing have him/her write for next week and then read it aloud.

Next Week's Assignment:

Read 2 Corinthians 3:17-18 and write your thoughts in your journal.

WEEK 15:
PAIN AND SHAME

In your opening prayer invite the Holy Spirit to come as the Healer of broken hearts.

God's Word

Read 2 Samuel 3:1-3 for your own information.

Have the group *read II Samuel 13 quietly*. Ask *what feelings this story brought out*. The leaders should be prepared for some emotional reactions to this passage.

Most people in our society define rape as a man, or men, forcing a girl or woman to participate in sexual intercourse. This story fits that description. The Bible also talks about men desiring to molest men (Judges 19).

Because sin was rampant we can assume that children of both genders were abused in many ways. In our day sexual abuse is a major problem. This type of wounding will usually manifest itself in later years by behaviors that reflect anger, shame, rejection, and a need to control others. It is not only a horrific act, but one that can alter the course of a life.

Other hurtful behaviors from early sexual exploitation include addictions, promiscuity, and depression.

This is a very sensitive subject that is extremely painful to share. Allow the Holy Spirit to guide you as you gently paraphrase the story of Tamar and discuss it.

Note Tamar's beauty and innocence. Was she guilty? Why, or why not?

She is depicted as young, innocent, and pure. She begged him not to do it.

What could she have done differently?

Because the king had told her to go to Amnon, she could not refuse. One did not disobey the king.

Was this a set-up? Considering that Amnon was her older brother and the heir apparent, should she have felt a sense of danger?

It was a set-up, but because of her innocence, Tamar would not have expected Amnon to have evil intentions. They had grown up together in the same family. He was her half-brother. He was the first born, the heir to the throne. She completely trusted him and probably looked up to him. She must have felt very special when Amnon requested her presence.

What type of love did Amnon have for Tamar?

Moving On

Lust. Note the description of love in I Corinthians 13:4-8. Instead of loving her, he actually plotted her downfall.

What counsel did he listen to?

An evil cousin who played on Amnon's pride.

What were his feelings after the rape?

Hate for her. Possible fear at the potential consequences of his actions.

See Leviticus 18:11. He could have received special dispensation to marry her, but all he wanted was to satisfy his own lust. His hate for her may have been a projection of his feelings of guilt onto her. "If I blame her I won't feel or look guilty". Note that she had no witnesses. Abusers transfer blame to their victims, making them feel guilty. (An example is an eight-year-old little girl who told her minister she had committed sexual sin.)

How did Tamar respond? Note that she did not hide her disgrace.

She left Amnon's house in tears and weeping loudly. This was a public walk of shame. Venting in an appropriate way is healthy.

Discuss her feelings of violation, betrayal of trust, sense of ruin, loss of dreams, confusion, aloneness, rejection, and being unworthy of love. How does this make them feel?

How does this story affect your feelings about hurtful situations you could not control?

Some may feel anger, others shame, and some fear. Remember, these are emotions and we need to allow ourselves to release emotions in a healthy way, such as journaling and sharing in group.

How did Absalom respond? See verses 28 and 29.

Typical family reaction, "Let's cover it up and pretend it never happened." This results in bitterness, masks, and other symptoms of dysfunction.

How did David respond?

He was furious but did nothing. How would Tamar have felt about that?

Why didn't her father do anything? See II Samuel, chapters 11 and 12.

This led to more tragedy. See II Samuel 13:28 and 29, and 18:33.

How do victims feel towards those who did not defend them?

People often feel more anger and betrayal towards the person who did not defend them than they feel towards the abuser.

Meeting Focus

Week 15: Pain And Shame

God gives us accounts in the Bible to help us deal with our feelings. What principles can we learn from this story? These might include confronting the abuser with truth even if they do not receive it, releasing the pain, going to someone we trust who can help us, and leaving the place of pain. In reading God's Word, and in sharing our pain, we grow in freedom and, therefore, healing.

How did this story in II Samuel 13 make you feel? This Biblical account may be difficult if you have been a victim of sexual assault. Remember, you were the victim. Now it is time to confront your abuse. Facing your feelings is painful, but it leads to healing. Journaling allows you to understand your own reactions better.

Encourage journaling.

Read 2 Corinthians 3:17-18 together. Ask everyone to share what they journaled about these verses. It's good to remember that regardless of the hurts we can walk in freedom. That freedom allows us to reflect Jesus and move in what He is leading us to do.

Next Week's Assignment:

1. *Journal on how the story of Tamar made you feel. Facing feelings and allowing oneself to actually feel the pain is very hard, but it is a key factor in the healing process. One idea is to write a fictional, but fact-based, story of your own abuse. You can also draw a picture and journal on it as in Week Seven.*

2. *Read the first three chapters of Nehemiah and answer the questions on your workbook page. It's a good idea to memorize Galatians 6:2.*

Take time to pray for and support those who are hurting. Be sure to follow up.

WEEK 16:
REBUILDING THE RUINS

Have you ever felt overwhelmed; that you had too many broken issues?

God's Word

Nehemiah heard of the desolation in Jerusalem, and it broke his heart. He lost his joy. There are just too many Christians surrounded by ruins, broken walls, broken dreams. When we focus on all of these negatives we become discouraged. Satan's lies start to sound true, and we feel our faith and joy seeping away. We can end up living an existence that falls short of the abundant life Jesus died to give us.

Read Nehemiah 1:1-3. Nehemiah needed to know what his countrymen were dealing with. In these verses we see people living among the ruins of a past glory. They could remember the good life, but all they could see was rubble. The enemy controlled their minds with shame and put-downs. They had no protection.

Discuss Nehemiah 1 by summarizing the chapter.

RUINS are those things that are the result of horrible pain in the past. These survivors were living in distress and reproach among old ruins. Sometimes victims even feel guilt over their "ruins". Some may be in denial about their past. The first step is to recognize a problem.

What ruins do you see in your life? Take some time to label your pains. Bring them out into the light of truth. Allow Jesus' love and the acceptance of others in the group or someone else you trust to encourage you to face each issue. Then you can begin to "look and live".

Tread softly. Some may not be as ready to deal with issues as they appear to be.

STRONGHOLDS are areas where Satan has established control. We are forgiven sinners growing in God. Sometimes we make mistakes. Sometimes we sin. In such cases we ask Jesus to forgive us, and He does (see 1 John 1:9). However, if there are areas where we cannot seem to get the victory we may be dealing with a foothold (Ephesians 4:27) or a stronghold (2 Corinthians 10:4).

Review the paper on "Defeating Sins". If you are struggling in an area, go back to where Satan got his foot in the door of your thoughts. Think about how that sin hurts you and the people you love. Renounce the sin and its effects. Then pray and order the enemy to leave and stay out in Jesus' Name.

WALLS represent ways that we hide. Do you have walls, or certain behaviors you hide behind?

What do you do when your defenses are gone?

Moving On

Remember, these people were former exiles. They and their fathers had suffered greatly. After many decades they had returned to their land, their royal city, and a new life of hope.

However, this was a place without walls, for the enemy had broken them down. Their defenses were gone. They were totally vulnerable to those around them who wanted to see them destroyed. In this case rebuilding the walls represents strength and protection, not that which keeps out healthy relationships. Why hadn't the exiles rebuilt the ruined walls?

According to Nehemiah 1:3 and 2:10 they were living in trouble and disgrace. This stole their sense of identity, their motivation and their faith in God.

What did Nehemiah do in verses 4-11?

He prayed a prayer that is an amazing example for us when we are in trouble.

This was not an easy prayer. It was not a comfortable prayer. Nehemiah was broken, and he went to the only One who could do anything about it. There are several elements in his prayer that we can learn from.

Nehemiah began by <u>recognizing</u> God. He worshipped God because God is powerful and mighty but also loving and full of mercy towards those who obey Him.

Then he <u>confessed</u> that the Israelites, and he and his family, had sinned terribly against God. But he also <u>reminded</u> God of God's promises to restore His people that repented and obeyed Him.

He finished with a <u>plea</u> for God to hear and give him favor with the king of Persia.

What a great example for us as we seek the Lord's help! He is all powerful, yet, all loving. On that basis we can confess our past sins, remind God of His promises, and ask for His favor as we continue to grow in His freedom.

Look at the second chapter of Nehemiah. Nehemiah won the king's favor because he already had the Heavenly King's favor. He went to Jerusalem and, in verse thirteen, he surveyed the damage. He did that with just a few trusted men. What a great example!

Take an honest look at your damaged areas, then start rebuilding with God's help and that of your brothers (or sisters) in the Lord.

Verse fourteen mentions a part of the wall that Nehemiah couldn't get through on his trip around the damaged walls. Sometimes a part may be too badly damaged to deal with right away. Let God direct you to the part to deal with first.

Hope was spoken and the people chose to move with what God wanted to do.

In Nehemiah, chapter 3, the people each did their share, working together for the benefit of all. That is "group"! We need other people to help us rebuild.

Week 16: Rebuilding The Ruins

Discuss Biblical principles for friendship. Look up Proverbs 17:17; 16:28; 27:6, 10; Luke 11:8; Romans 15:1; Ephesians 4:2; and Colossians 3:13.

Read the following verse together:

> *Bear (endure, carry) one another's burdens and troublesome moral faults, and in this way fulfill and observe perfectly the law of Christ (the Messiah) and complete what is lacking [in your obedience to it]. - Galatians 6:2 (AMPC)*

Meeting Focus

Think about possible walls in your life. Are they good walls that help you establish boundaries, or are they walls to hide behind?

Next Week's Assignment

1. *Read the rest of Nehemiah. Come next week prepared to share one truth from the book of Nehemiah that you can apply to your situation. Journal on that truth.*

2. *From Nehemiah, chapter four, write down some principles that will help you defeat opposition and discouragement.*

3. *Memorize Galatians 6:2.*

4. *What was the result of Nehemiah's perseverance in verse sixteen of chapter six?*

5. *Journal on past pains that were identified today.*

WEEK 17:
DEALING WITH NEGATIVE WORDS

God's Word

Your family and friends may be very supportive of your journey to healing. If that is the case you are most fortunate. At other times family and friends will mock changes they see you trying to make, deny events from your past, and try to come against your efforts to receive healing. Why do you think they might do that?

People who are living in sin are convicted by righteous living. The enemy also uses people, even well-meaning people, to block the healing that God is doing.

Satan will try to condemn you. The difference between Satan and God is that Satan condemns us and pours shame and feelings of failure on us. God through the work of the Holy Spirit convicts us to bring us close to Himself. Remember, Jesus brings life (John 3:16-21).

We need to understand that we must always be ready to deal with spiritual opposition. See Ephesians 6:10-20. How strongly do you want to see your healing become a reality?

Look at the fourth chapter of Nehemiah. Some mocked Nehemiah and tried to block his success. Why did they do this?

They were used to being in control and they had great contempt for the Jews. (4:1-3)

According to verse 6, what do you need to do to be successful?

We must have a mindset to do the work. It helps to have someone like Nehemiah in our lives to inspire and encourage us.

Set your entire spirit towards the process. It takes focus with a purpose.

In verses 8 and 9, Nehemiah and his men sought God. Pray and be alert to prepare yourself for possible ploys of Satan. Some people will not even recognize they are being used by the enemy to discourage you. Put on the whole armor of God Paul writes about in Ephesians 6. Our weapons are the Word of God and prayer.

We can stand!!!

Discouragement came to the leaders when they looked at the whole problem. It was just too much! Focus on one issue at a time. Let others you trust help you. And, remember that your healing affects others. It's worth working for. We can gain spiritual support from each other.

In Nehemiah 6:16, the work was completed. God was glorified and future generations reaped the benefits. The final outcome in Nehemiah 8:10 was joy as God gave them His strength. He will do the same for each person who asks Him.

Moving On

Meeting Focus

Are other people affected by your pain?

What are your goals?

What steps do you need to take to move forward?

What is at stake?

Next Week's Assignment:

1. Journal on your goals and what steps you will have to take to reach them.

2. Journal on any remaining issues you may have been avoiding.

3. Read the Word!

WEEK 18:
HEALTHY CONFRONTATION

The Merriam-Webster Dictionary defines confrontation as "a face to face meeting; the clashing of forces or ideas; or comparison". In Victory's Journey we use the term, "compassionately confrontational". Jesus was confrontational. He challenged people from where they were to follow Him into a new life. Even though at times Jesus was very strong, He loved people! He had compassion.

To most of us the word confrontation is unpleasant. What does it mean to you?

Think about a confrontation you had in the past. How did it turn out?

What are some principles to keep in mind when you feel you need to confront someone?

1. Know the <u>issues</u>.

2. Know <u>yourself</u> and your <u>motives</u>.

3. Know the other <u>person</u>. Treat them with respect.

4. Use <u>kind</u> words.

5. Seek a good solution that will help everyone.

God's Word

Have you ever heard of a daughter named Noah?

The story of Noah and her sisters is in Numbers 26:33 and 27:1-7. Here we see an example of positive confrontation. Note that the girls' father was Zelophehad. They had no rights because of their father's sin. Yet, they chose to confront those who were in authority that could help them. Do you think that took a lot of courage?

In this case confrontation is not a bad word, for they came with a good attitude. God honored them. It seems they had some idea of God's grace and justice.

Meeting Focus

Think of some positive and some negative ways to confront others.

<u>Positive:</u>

After prayer

With a soft voice

Moving On

Talk about your feelings; be open to their feelings and opinions

<u>Negative:</u>

With a tone of shouting or shaming or accusing

In a superior or judgmental way

Without allowing them to express their feelings

Nehemiah confronted the king, but he did it in a humble non-aggressive manner. Esther is a good example of preparing for the confrontation with prayer and seeking God. Notice her attitude of respect and the wisdom in which she set the stage for her confrontation. She did her part, and God made some other things "just seem to happen". Victory was the end result.

Next Week's Assignment

1. Journal on people and situations which have hurt you. Write letters to those who caused the pain, using healthy confrontational approaches. In the letter(s) state what happened and how it made you feel. Delegate the blame to the appropriate person. If you are guilty for any of it, confess that. Recognize that the one behind it all was Satan.

Put these letters aside. You will complete them next week.

This may cause some very emotional reactions. Remind the members that you are available if they need to call you.

NOTE: <u>Do not send the letters at this time!</u> *These letters should **<u>only</u>** be delivered after praying about it with your leaders and as the Holy Spirit leads. Even if they are never read by the hurtful party, there is healing in the writing and the praying over them. Some people may want to read them in group, give them to the leaders, burn them, or just put them away in their Bibles.*

2. Start a praise journal of thank you messages to God for things, people, Scriptures, and situations that have helped you.

WEEK 19:
FORGIVENESS

In the past, your ability to make good choices may have been affected by things like distrust, shame, anger, fear, and self-pity. As we grow in Christ it is crucial that we learn how to make the right choices.

God's Word

Read Psalm 124:6 & 7 and Psalm 91:3.

> *Praise be to the LORD, who has not let us be torn by their teeth. We have escaped like a bird out of the fowler's snare; the snare has been broken, and we have escaped. -Psalm 124:6-7*

> *Surely he will save you out of the fowler's snare and from the deadly pestilence. - Psalm 91:3*

What snare does God want to help us escape?

We make a choice when we face our fears and anger and any other issues we may be dealing with. Trusting God completely is difficult if you have trusted people that have hurt you. It is good to remember our lessons on God. He is faithful and trustworthy. He loves us unconditionally. While that does not mean He gives us everything we ask for when we want it, it does mean He gives us what we need when we need it. Stepping away from the snares of the enemy means stepping into the Truth of God's Word. It means choosing to listen to the positive thoughts and words in life. It means rejecting the lies and negative concepts that Satan wants us to believe.

It also means choosing to forgive. While forgiveness is a process that God has to help us work through, we must begin by an act of our will. We must decide to forgive. Forgiveness is not a denial of the pain. It does not mean trusting. It does mean not living in the hurt. When we forgive someone we erase the list of their sins against us and we free them to receive Christ's forgiveness. Trust, on the other hand, must be earned. It may take time to rebuild. As we grow the Lord will give us more wisdom in our trusting. Hurts are a part of life, but God can help you forgive. (That does not mean you will never be hurt again, although, as you heal, you will be less vulnerable to those who are looking for someone to hurt.)

Write down the name(s) of anyone you know you need to forgive.

Moving On

Ask if there are specific people that anyone needs to forgive. You can take time for everyone to write their names in their notebook.

Some may also be angry at God. That is okay. God can take it, and He will help them understand that He loved them and has brought them to this place of healing.

Jesus tells us that if we want to be forgiven we must forgive others. He never asks us to do the impossible, so that means He will help us. God loves you and has brought you to this place of healing. It is the enemy, Satan, who was behind all of the destruction, and he is the one we fight against. The joyful truth is that in fighting Satan, we are victorious through Christ.

> *For though we walk (live) in the flesh, we are not carrying on our warfare according to the flesh and using mere human weapons. For the weapons of our warfare are not physical [weapons of flesh and blood], but they are mighty before God for the overthrow and destruction of strongholds, [Inasmuch as we] refute arguments and theories and reasonings and every proud and lofty thing that sets itself up against the [true] knowledge of God; and we lead every thought and purpose away captive into the obedience of Christ (the Messiah, the Anointed One) - 2 Corinthians 10:3-5 (AMPC)*

And that is just what we must do. We must each decide to put every negative thought in a box and throw it into the deepest part of the Sea of God's Forgetfulness, <u>and ours</u>. We must deny any proud and false thoughts access into our thinking. Instead, we must fill our minds and hearts with worship to our wonderful Bridegroom, Jesus Christ, who loves us unconditionally. Let us choose to think and speak in a positive way. Let us choose not to swim in shame and pain but to soar on wings as eagles. Read Philippians 4:8 and I Corinthians 13, especially verses 4 to 8.

God can also help you to leave behind your hurts and move into the blessings and the life He has planned for you. (Read Jeremiah 29:11.) So many people say they want to be free of the past, but they still want to carry around suitcases filled with negative thinking, bitter attitudes, and hurtful behavior. Just remember, we also have God's joy and strength to help us to deal with our hurts.

Read Deuteronomy 28:1-13 and 30:19-20 and name the blessings God wants to give His people. You might want to underline them in your Bible.

What does God want us to choose?

Life! It is the reward for obedience.

What have you been choosing?

Week 19: Forgiveness

Meeting Focus

Review your identity in Christ (see Week 10).

Lead the members in a discussion of who each person is in Christ. We are forgiven, made righteous, joint heirs with Jesus, and adopted as children of God for starters. How does God see each individual?

What gifts and personality traits has God given you?

What good qualities and talents does each one have? (Be prepared ahead of time through prayer and meditation to list several positives about each one.)

How can you use them to bless others?

Now talk about the specific areas that we all need to work on (for example, courage and hope). Ask the group if they would like to share an area they need to give extra attention to. Stop and pray for each one of them. Ask the Lord to help each person see himself (or herself) as God sees him/her. Encourage them to give God permission to do what He needs to do to heal them and change them into the people He wants them to be.

Next Week's Assignment

1. *Write God a letter, giving Him your memories, pain, shame, anger, walls, and vulnerability. (Note 1 Peter 5:7.) Renounce their effect on you.*

2. *Pray, asking God to help you release your past pains to Him. Ask Him to help you receive God's love and the love and acceptance of godly people.*

3. *Take out the letters you wrote last week. Write letters to anyone else you still need to forgive. Tell them how they hurt you, how that felt, and how it has affected you. At the end of each letter tell them that Jesus has forgiven you, and you are choosing to forgive them. Please do not send these letters until you and your leaders have prayed over them. If it would do more damage to send them you should destroy them. Your purpose is healing, not revenge.*

4. *Journal about your future hopes and dreams. Replace "self-talk" with "Word-talk". Choose life!*

5. *Read Luke 11:21-23, Romans 8 and 12 and Ephesians 4:1-5:21.*

You may need to do some checking up on each member this week.

WEEK 20:
HEALTHY RELATIONSHIPS

Healthy relationships don't just happen; they take work. Fill in the chart below.

God's Word

Luke 11:21-23, Romans 8 & 12, and Ephesians 4:1-5:21 are passages that teach us godly character traits. (Remember, we can only make choices for ourselves, not others.)

You may want to make a chart on poster board of the things that destroy and the things that build relationships. This may help cement these truths. The group members can add things that help a relationship to be healthy.

Things that destroy relationships include put-downs, dishonesty, desertion, criticism, rejection, selfishness, and doing the wrong type of things together.

Things that build include love, shared laughter, appreciation, talking together about God and His Word, prayer, fun times, sharing on a feeling level, and doing kind deeds of ministry together.

As your group reviews Luke 11:21-23, Romans 8 & 12, and Ephesians 4:1-5:21, use your poster board chart to add the things we need to get rid of and the things we need to develop as Christians. Review blind spots and strongholds from Week Nine.

THINGS THAT DESTROY	THINGS THAT BUILD

Moving On

Meeting Focus

In learning how to be all we can be, we need to understand the root causes of why we react the way we do. Draw a chart of this progression of negative reactions. You may have some other things you can add.

- *Rejection, either real or perceived, leads to hurt feelings.*

- *When we are hurt we feel like a failure and may develop a crushed spirit.*

- *That crushed spirit can lead to self-pity, if we allow it.*

- *From self-pity, resentment towards the person who we feel caused our pain blossoms into resistance and arguing, even with other people.*

- *Our resentment causes us to keep records of the wrongs done to us. Unreal expectations lead to anger when these expectations are not met.*

- *Unresolved pain and anger pushes us to react to anything that triggers those old feelings, even if we do not recognize the similarity.*

- *Eventually, we isolate ourselves from God and others.*

You can make it personal by writing in specific situations.

Many people allow God to heal them from past issues only to fall into Satan's snare with a current relationship issue. Our enemy desires nothing more than to put us back into bondage. The principles we learn in this program are not meant to just help with the old issues; they are tools that will help with new issues as well. Learn them well and make them a part of how you handle life.

Developing healthy relational habits takes time and conscious effort. The wonderful truth is that as we do our part God will do His. One point to remember is that this life has its thorns. Thorns are not bad things. Rather, they are a means of growth to those who will learn by them. We may fail and others may fail us but if we follow the characteristics to healthy relationships we will win.

As the group members heal, they need to develop healthy relationship habits. The Scripture passages in this lesson give great suggestions for a place to start. The truth is that the more time we spend with people the more we tend to be like them. Spending time with Jesus is the best way to have the best handle on dealing with relationships. Let Him be your best Friend!

Week 20: Healthy Relationships

Next Week's Assignment

1. Journal on any remaining areas of difficulty.

2. List some areas that you can work on to develop good relationship habits.

Close in a prayer time that allows everyone to gather around each person and pray for them individually.

WEEK 21:
CHANGE

Lana and her family struggled with alcohol addiction. They attended church, but the old life and its habits were too much of a stronghold for them to break free from on their own. Then came the day when Lana decided she needed help. She wanted a new beginning for herself and her children. Jesus set her free. The old desires were gone. She had hope and a future.

It just so happened that Lana's mother lived down the street. It was their habit to get together every day for a drink and a visit. Lana told her mom that she was different, that she was free and wanted to stay that way. But every day when she stopped in to see her, her mom put a drink in front of her. Why would a mother purposely undermine her child's good decisions?

Many people feel more guilt and conviction when they see someone break free from old habits. As long as Lana was drinking with her, her mom could rationalize that her habit wasn't so bad. Remember Nehemiah's enemies.

God's Word

In most cases change is good and everyone is glad for it, but it can carry a price tag. Some people that you have been close to in the past may not like the "new" changes and may actually sabotage your efforts to become all God wants you to be. Some family members and friends may want you to continue to be weak and vulnerable, or they may want you to keep the old "masks" and not rock the boat. A few spouses will be uncomfortable with the changes in your devotion and dependence on Christ Jesus. Some may feel left out or unsure of how they fit into the picture now.

What are some situations you see in your own life?

Jesus said that we must take up our cross and follow Him. Read Matthew 10:29-39 and notice:

1. *Your value – verses 29-31*

2. *Your responsibility before God and its effect – verses 32-33*

3. *Possible reactions from people who are not God-seekers – verses 34-36*

4. *The love-priority – verse 37-38*

5. *The reward – verse 39*

Meeting Focus

Does this mean we brush our loved ones off and fail to love and minister to them?

Read 1 Peter 3:1-16. We have a responsibility to live in our Christian freedom in such a way that

Moving On

others will want it, too. Then we know we have done our best with God's help, and the choice becomes theirs. The Holy Spirit helps us do this for in ourselves we are weak. In fact, we are just getting used to this life of freedom and joy!

What are some practical things we can do to help difficult situations?

Lana had to talk with her mom and tell her that, even though she loved her and wanted to spend time together, she couldn't do that if her mother insisted on trying to get her to drink with her. That was a healthy boundary. She reinforced this conversation with expressions of love. Her mom mocked her new stance but eventually began to respect her.

An important guideline - be kind in word and in action. Pray for the people in your family or at work. Some may respond and accept the new you. Some may even want to know more about how you changed.

If those you have been close to refuse to support you, you may need to back off. That does not mean that you destroy any bridges to them. It does mean you must be sure that you are putting Jesus first. Most of all, remember that God loves our loved ones more than we do. We have wonderful promises in God's Word to hold onto. Consider these verses as you pray for your loved ones:

> *Do not be anxious about anything, but in every situation, by prayer and petition, with thanksgiving, present your requests to God. And the peace of God, which transcends all understanding, will guard your hearts and your minds in Christ Jesus.*
>
> *Finally, brothers, whatever is true, whatever is noble, whatever is right, whatever is pure, whatever is lovely, whatever is admirable--if anything is excellent or praiseworthy--think about such things.........And the God of peace will be with you. - Philippians 4:6-9*
>
> *Nothing will be impossible for you.- Matthew 17:20*

As you close in prayer pray for each person's home situation. Ask God to help the group members change their attitudes towards themselves and others. Pray for the Lord to build up their confidence in Him.

WEEK 22:
BOUNDARIES

Pray Galatians 5:1:

> *It is for freedom that Christ has set us free. Stand firm, then, and do not let yourselves be burdened again by a yoke of slavery.*

Pray:

Dear Lord, thank you for the freedom you bought us with your precious blood when You died on the cross. We accept that freedom in every area of our lives. Help us to stand firmly in it and not give in to Satan's tricks to pull us back into slavery to old thought patterns and behaviors. In Jesus' name, Amen (so be it)!

God's Word

Boundaries are good. Without them our world and our lives would be total chaos. Let's look at God as the One who knows the value of boundaries.

> *Who shut up the sea behind doors when it burst forth from the womb, when I made the clouds its garment and wrapped it in thick darkness, when I fixed limits for it and set its doors and bars in place, when I said, 'This far you may come and no farther; here is where your proud waves halt"? -Job 38:8-11*

What is the key thought in this passage?

Limits are good!

God is not a God of confusion but of order. One of the proofs of the existence of a Supreme Being is the order of the universe. *He ordained boundaries in nature. Without those limits we would have constant upheaval; with them we have beauty.*

What do the following passages tell us?

> *When the Most High gave the nations their inheritance, when he divided all mankind, he set up boundaries for the peoples according to the number of the sons of Israel. - Deuteronomy 32:8*

> *From one man he made all the nations, that they should inhabit the whole earth; and he marked out their appointed times in history and the boundaries of their lands. - Acts 17:26*

The locale and the times of the nations are set within God's specific calendar. It is interesting that the fall of nations is usually, if not always, preceded by moral decline.

Moving On

> *A person's days are determined; you have decreed the number of his months and have set limits he cannot exceed. - Job 14:5*

> *The boundary lines have fallen for me in pleasant places; surely I have a delightful inheritance. - Psalm 16:6*

God has set boundaries for nature, nations, and for human beings. Boundaries have to do with a divine plan and purpose. It is His desire to bless us and to help us fulfill all the purpose He has ordained for us. David said that God's personal boundaries for him were pleasant.

Looking at all of these Scriptures we can agree with what Mordecai told Queen Esther in Esther 4:14.

> *For if you remain silent at this time, relief and deliverance for the Jews will arise from another place, but you and your father's family will perish. And who knows but that you have come to royal position for such a time as this? - Esther 4:14*

How might that be true of your life?

We looked at Joshua's promises and choices in the beginning of our journey together. Let's reread Joshua 1:1-9.

God gave Joshua a specific calling to lead His people into the Promised Land. He established the boundaries of the area that belonged to the Israelites, but Joshua and the people had to claim those boundaries by walking them out.

What does God want to do in your life along these lines? Is there a "land" you need to take possession of? It could be an area where you are still struggling, a relationship, or a promise for your future.

With Joshua's call came promises. What were these promises in verses 3, 5, 7 and 8?

How can you walk out the promises God has given you?

The ultimate promise of success was based on God's <u>Presence</u> being with Joshua. God also promised that along that journey no one would be able to stand against him and his God-given authority.

There were also some things Joshua had to do. What were they in verses 6-9?

Week 22: Boundaries

What actions must you take to receive God's promises?

How courageous are you when you meet opposition or temptation? What can you do to improve your courage level?

Meeting Focus

People who have been hurt by other people struggle with healthy boundaries. They may make the boundaries around them like walls so people cannot get too close. Usually these people try to control their environment and the people who they have relationships with because then they feel safe. In so doing they intrude on the boundaries of others.

On the other hand, they may not have any protective walls. In that case they are so anxious to please that they lose their identity and their God-given purpose.

Read Romans 12:2. Are we to change our personal identity to please other people?

God wants us to let our mindset be changed to the pattern of Christ (Philippians 2:5-11). That means knowing who we are and whose we are.

Healthy personal boundaries happen when you know who you are, and you treat yourself and others with respect. You know you are created by God with <u>unique</u> qualities that are good and that He loves you. (Knowing He loves you as you are helps you love others as they are.) Remember love is not a lack of boundaries.

God wants us to feel free to say yes or no without guilt, anger, or fear. Having Christ's mindset will help us know when to say "yes" and when to say "no". It will also release you from false guilt or guilt another person is trying to put on you.

What are some practical ways you can set boundaries in your life?

Seek God at the beginning of each day. Ask the Holy Spirit to give you wisdom, discernment, and love. Set your priorities. Plan ahead how you will spend your time. Know your spiritual goals. Know what is too much for you to handle.

One way to deal with those who step on your boundaries is take time to think about the situation. Use the time to figure out how you really feel and how to express it. Write your thoughts down on paper. Then do it. It won't be easy, but you'll feel free and strong (and a little guilty at first) – and it will get easier. Always ask, "What would Jesus do!" He set positive boundaries and He loved at the same time. We can follow His example.

Moving On

Another area is to set boundaries against the enemy's temptations and attacks. Because you have been given authority in Christ (Ephesians 1:19-21) you can determine what areas are off limits to Satan. Of course, you must stand your ground after that decision has been made!

Next Week's Assignment

1. Journal on areas where you struggle to maintain safe and godly boundaries.

2. Make a list of things you can do to stand firmly in your freedom.

> *Do not be anxious about anything, but in every situation by prayer and petition, with thanksgiving, present your requests to God. And the peace of God, which transcends all understanding, will guard your hearts and your minds in Christ Jesus -Philippians 4:6-7*

No one can take your joy unless you let them!

WEEK 23:
COMPLETE SURRENDER

This has been quite a journey as we have looked at a variety of people in the Bible and examined our own similar issues. It is my prayer that you have seen victory in a number of areas as you have released these areas to God. God is going to complete the work in you as you continually give Him permission to do so.

God's Word

There is a final major key to unlocking the door of freedom spiritually and emotionally. That key is complete surrender to the Savior who carried our sin and pain, and who now sits on the right hand of the Father making intercession for us.

Read Luke 7:36-50 and think about how you might feel if you'd been the uninvited guest at this special dinner party given in Christ's honor. The guests included the rich and famous in town.

Whose home was Jesus in?

He was in the home of Simon, a Pharisee.

What kind of a woman entered the room?

She was known in that town as a sinful woman.

What was the reaction?

Simon thought that Jesus lacked discernment. Others in the room saw her as unclean. They were probably doing a lot of whispering and eye-rolling.

How did she react to the people who were discussing her sins?

She didn't because her focus was entirely on Jesus.

Because her focus was completely on Jesus she was not pulled down by the voices and looks of those around her. She was intentional!

Many people who have found freedom in Christ are still seeking approval from a person who seems important to them. If that is our focus we will miss the great thrill of pouring our love on Jesus and receiving His love and approval. The others judged her as a sinner. Was it because her very presence there reminded them of their own failures?

Some Pharisees were believers. Can Christians have the wrong attitudes?

Yes, because they are carrying their own baggage.

How should we respond to those who attack us?

Moving On

We need to remember we belong to Jesus and He loves us and knows how valuable we are. Because of that we do not cringe and fall into slavery to those who want to control us. On the other hand the Bible tells us how we are to respond to people who mistreat us.

Here are some Scriptures to remind us of how to respond:

My dear brothers and sisters, take note of this: Everyone should be quick to listen, slow to speak and slow to become angry. -James 1:19

Who is wise and understanding among you? Let him show it by his good life, by deeds done in the humility that comes from wisdom. But if you harbor bitter envy and selfish ambition in your hearts, do not boast about it or deny the truth. Such "wisdom" does not come down from heaven but is earthly, unspiritual, demonic. For where you have envy and selfish ambition, there you find disorder and every evil practice. But the wisdom that comes from heaven is first of all pure; then peace-loving, considerate, submissive, full of mercy and good fruit, impartial and sincere. Peacemakers who sow in peace raise a harvest of righteousness.- James 3:13-18

A gentle answer turns away wrath, but a harsh word stirs up anger. - Proverbs 15:1

God wants us to love even those who are hateful to us. As we ask the Holy Spirit to guide our thoughts and words He will help us answer in a kind way but also in a wise way.

This woman had a shameful past. Jesus asked, "Do you see this woman?"

Pause and let that thought sink in. You might ask them to close their eyes and bow their heads as they consider this question.

Do you see her? Are you like this woman? Notice her tears, her love, and her extravagant service. Notice the Lord's response to her. Do you believe Jesus responds to you with approval?

What do you need to change in your mindset to have such surrender?

She comes, knowing that the One Who matters will not condemn her. She brings her all, trusting Him completely with her most precious item. She gives Him all that she has left of herself that is undefiled. Do you see the richness of that? She did not give Him the leftovers, the dirty parts, the thing that was easy to release. She gave her most valued possession, her only valued possession, and she gave it in a way that she could not take it back. She became radical in her devotion. She broke the alabaster box!

People often hold back from giving Jesus everything because of fear. But, remember, He is not going to make worse decisions for you than you would make even if you could see from His divine perspective. He loved this woman with all her faults and He received her gift. Not only that, He gave her the gift of forgiveness. She died to herself that day at His feet in front of all of the judgmental witnesses, but she stood up in newness of life.

Meeting Focus

What was this woman's key to freedom?

She had an absolute love that produced total submission.

She came in total humility and extreme love. She traded the old for the new. She expressed her love for Jesus with a personal sacrifice, a broken alabaster box pouring out expensive myrrh, a symbol of death. Jesus loved her with His sacrifice, a broken body, pouring out His precious blood, a symbol of life. It is interesting that when she walked away she still carried the fragrance in her hair. Jesus always gives us something beautiful when we give Him that which costs us much.

How can you give your love to Jesus?

Ask if it is hard for some of them to just reach out and accept His gift.

Christ calls us. He offers His gifts of life, freedom, and worth. But it isn't a one-time experience; it is a daily walking with Him in His approval until we do not even hear the voices that would tear us down. It is keeping focused on our love-relationship with our precious Lord!

That is how Philippians 1:6 works! He completes the work in us as we stay close to Him because we love Him.

Have each one write on a small slip (or slips) of paper what they feel they need to surrender as a sacrifice to Jesus, the One who loves them so much.

Pray and give whatever you are holding onto to Jesus Christ in a time of total release and surrender to His Lordship. Total surrender involves total release of our belongings, our reputation, our family, ourselves.

Pray over each one after they have prayed a prayer of release.

Remind them to bring their envelope with the "Personal Evaluation" they did early in the group for next week's class. You may want to have everyone bring snacks for a celebration.

WEEK 24:
VICTORY!

This would be a great time to celebrate what God has done in your life. Completing this program does not mean you will never face difficult situations again. It does mean that you have tools to be victorious.

Do the repeat "Personal Evaluation". Then open the one you did at the beginning of the program and compare your answers. What do you notice that is different?

Take testimonies.

God promises great things for those who overcome. One promise is that we will be given a white stone with a new name written on it (Revelation 2:17). You are a special overcomer and you can be proud of the hard work you have done. God has great things ahead and with your new mindset you can move forward in God's favor. Remember, God is still at work, and He will continue to help complete His purpose for you until the day He calls you to Himself.

Go forward in victory! This is not the end; it is the beginning of a new life!

Journaling is a good habit to continue.

Remind them of this as you gather all of their journals and pray over them, asking God to cover everything written there with His love. Pray for protection from Satan's traps and for success and favor as they move in their new freedom.

Ask them to fill out the "Please write on…" questions.

Those who still need to work through some issues can join another group or receive individual counseling. You can continue with them by working through a book such as "*Victory Over the Darkness*" and doing some of the additional suggestions at the back of this manual.

They have worked hard over the past months. It's time to have a special ceremony. You might invite the ministry leadership to join you. (Be sure the whole group is okay with that.) You might break bread together and give each person a personal Scripture verse. A white rose is also a lovely gift for ladies.

This is the time to hand out completion certificates. Referring to the section on "Closure" and the "Victory's Journey Progression", review what this journey has covered. Talk about the transition from a victim, overcome with the pains of the past, to a person of God's Word, living an overcoming and victorious life. Let them know you are pleased with them. Whatever God has produced in them they are further in their victory journey.

Hand out a white stone with a Scripture reference on it. Philippians 1:6 is a great reminder

Moving On

of the victories they have won. These references can be painted on the stone with a gold paint pen. The white stone was a symbol of victory that was a key to favor.

Remind them to pray for one another and to keep in touch with a card or call. Strong bonds have united them while they are in the group. Just like siblings grow up and leave home, they will always have the memory of what they have shared together. Even if they do not see each other regularly, they will always be family.

Also, remind them that <u>the pledge of confidentiality</u> still holds. That is one of their love gifts to each other. Prayer is another gift! This is not the end; it is the beginning of a new life!

Plan a get-together in the next two or three weeks. Serve refreshments.

Our next gathering will be on _____ **at** _____.

Close with prayer over each of your group members.

Week 24: Victory

Please write on...................

1. What changes have I experienced since I started "Victory's Journey"?

2. What special memories do I have from the group?

3. Where am I on the "Victory's Journey Progression"?

4. What fears do I still need to work through?

5. Where am I spiritually?

6. What are my hopes and future plans?

SECTION 6:
MINISTRY HELPS

Additional Topics for Journaling and Sharing

1. Earliest memories and what you felt at the time

2. Memories of mother and/or father

3. Memories of each sibling (If none, write on effect that had on you.)

4. Bring in childhood pictures. Share with group. Notice expressions, eyes, family position and posture.

5. Person, place, or thing that causes a fear reaction (unexplained anxiety)

6. Emotions such as shame, rejection

7. Specific times you've felt alone, rejected

8. What you like about yourself. What others like about you.

9. How you think God views you. (Is this true according to the Word?)

10. Memory gaps (Be cautious of pulling out "false memories".)

11. Disappointments

12. Recurring feelings, smells, thoughts (What triggers these?)

13. Write your "life story" and read it in a group meeting.

14. List the things you say to yourself. (Discuss "self-talk" versus "Word-talk".)

15. Draw a picture of your family. (Note positions of family members in your picture. It may equal your view of them. Why did you view them there? Was that realistic?)

16. Draw a picture of your house (Are there ways to get in and out? Is it a pleasant scene? What do you see when you look at this picture?)

17. How you feel when you do something well or when you "mess-up"

18. Draw a time line of your life. Put happy memories on top of the line and painful memories on bottom. Then pick a painful memory and trace it forward to your goal.

      Ex. pain——————/————————/————————/—————goal
                        steps taken present need to do
                                (be specific)

References and Recommended Reading

Corey, Marianne Schneider & Gerald, (1997). Groups: Process and Practice. Pacific Grove, CA: Brooks/Cole Publishing.

Seamands, David A., (1985). Healing of Memories. Wheaton, IL: Victor Books

Dobbins, Richard D., (1982). Your Spiritual and Emotional Power. Old Tappan, NJ: Fleming H. Revell Company

Frank, Jan, (1987). A Door of Hope. San Bernardino, CA: Here's Life Publishers.

Meyer, Joyce, (1995). Battlefield of the Mind. Tulsa, OK: Harrison House

Cochrane, Linda, & Ficht, Susan, (1994). A Time to Heal. Valley Publishing.

Corey, Marianne Schneider & Gerald, (1993). Becoming a Helper. Pacific Grove, CA: Brooks/Cole Publishing.

Allen, LaRue, & Santrock, John W., (1993). Psychology: The Contexts of Behavior. Dubuque, PA: Wm. C. Brown & Benchmark Publishing.

Anderson, Neil T., (1990). Victory Over the Darkness. Ventura, CA: Regal Books

Anderson, Neil T., (2003). Discipleship Counseling. Ventura, CA: Regal Books.

Kendall, R.T., (2002). Total Forgiveness. Lake Mary, FL: Charisma House.

Clinton, Dr. Tim, (2006). Turn Your Life Around. New York, NY: Faith Words - Hatchette Book Group USA.

Hart, Archibald D., (2001). Unmasking Male Depression. W Publishing Group (A Division of Thomas Nelson, Inc.).

Hegstrom, Paul, (2004). Angry Men And the Women Who Love Them. Kansas City, MO: Beacon Hill Press of Kansas City.

Hegstrom, Paul, (2006). Broken Children, Grown Up Pain. Kansas City, MO: Beacon Hill Press of Kansas City.

Section 6: Ministry Helps

Victory's Journey

...offering help for today and hope for tomorrow.

Member Contract

Name_____ (please print)

I have been informed of and fully understand the process, goals and purpose of Victory's Journey, specifically its Biblical-based method for guiding participants in how to live the abundant life promised by Jesus. With such knowledge, I willingly choose to face the pains of my past by participating in the program and receiving the support of Victory's Journey leaders and other participants. With God's help, I commit myself to the difficult work necessary to promote the healing of past pains and conflicts.

As I become a participant in this program, I promise to maintain the confidentiality of all others in the ministry, recognizing the role absolute trust and safety play in the successful completion of this process. I will treasure their trust in me and view it as a gift.

I further understand that the Victory's Journey leaders are not mental health professionals. I acknowledge that I am not receiving professional treatment by participating in this program. I give my permission for group leaders to seek direction from a pastor or a mental health professional in the event that they have reasonable concerns regarding my welfare or the welfare of any other person(s) I may affect.

Because I understand that the group leaders and other participants are not licensed mental health professionals, I acknowledge that any counsel received by them will be that of a caring friend. Therefore, I assume any responsibility for any actions I take based on their advice. I release Victory's Journey Ministries, the sponsoring church and its leadership, and my individual group leaders and participants from any and all claims of responsibility and liability, legal or otherwise, that I, or any other person representing me, may have against them for counsel and advice given to me.

Signed: _____ Date: _____

Witnessed _____

"For I know the plans I have for you," declares the LORD, "plans to prosper you and not to harm you, plans to give you hope and a future." ......Jeremiah 29:11

Moving On

Victory's Journey

...offering help for today and hope for tomorrow.

Parent Contract

Child's Name _____ (please print)

Name _____ (please print)

I have been informed of and fully understand the process, goals and purpose of Victory's Journey, specifically its Biblical-based method for guiding participants in how to live the abundant life promised by Jesus. With such knowledge, I willfully and knowingly consent to my child's involvement in the program, as well as to their interaction with Victory's Journey leaders and other participants. With God's help, I will encourage my child to do the work necessary to promote the healing of past pains and conflicts.

I further understand that the Victory's Journey leaders are not mental health professionals. I acknowledge that my child shall not be receiving professional treatment throughout the course of the program. I give my permission for his/her group leaders to seek direction from a pastor or a mental health professional in the event that they have reasonable concerns regarding his/her welfare or the welfare of any other person(s) that may be affected.

Because I understand that the group leaders and other participants are not licensed mental health professionals, I acknowledge that any counsel received by them will be that of a caring friend. Therefore, I release Victory's Journey Ministries, the sponsoring church and its leadership, and my child's individual group leaders and participants from any and all claims of responsibility and liability, legal or otherwise, that I or my child, or any other person representing me or my child, may have against them for counsel and advice given to him/her.

Signed: _____ Date: _____

Witnessed _____

"For I know the plans I have for you," declares the LORD, "plans to prosper you and not to harm you, plans to give you hope and a future." ......Jeremiah 29:11

Section 6: Ministry Helps

Parental Consent and Release Form

I, _____, the undersigned parent or guardian of _____, hereby consent to my child participating in the Victory's Journey Ministries Group to be held on _____(day of week) from _____ until _____. I certify that my child is able and willing to participate in the program. If my child has any medical conditions and/or is on any medications that would affect his/her involvement in Victory's Journey Ministries and/or his/her progress in that program, I have listed them at the bottom of this form.

I understand and hereby agree to assume all of the risks that may be encountered as a result of my child's participation in the Victory's Journey group, including activities preliminary and subsequent thereto. I do hereby agree to hold _____ (church) and its agents and employees, harmless from any and all liabilities, legal or otherwise, including but not limited to actions, causes of actions, claims, expenses and fees, defense costs, attorney fees and damages on account of injury to my child or property, even injury resulting in death, which I now have or which may arise in the future in connection with the activities or participation in any other activities associated with participation in this program.

I expressly agree that this release, waiver and indemnity agreement is intended to be broad and inclusive as permitted and governed by the laws of the State of Pennsylvania and that if any portion thereof is held invalid, it is agreed that the balance shall, notwithstanding, continue in full legal force and effect. This release contains the entire agreement between the parties hereto and the terms of this release are contractual and not a mere recital.

I further state that I have carefully read the foregoing release and know the contents thereof, and I sign this release as my own free act. This is a legally binding agreement which I have read and understand.

_____ _____
Parent or Guardian   Date

_____ _____
Witness   Date

Emergency contact information:

_____

Medical Information:

Moving On

Confidential Personal History

Name _____ Telephone _____

Address _____

_____

Were your parents Christians? Did they live their profession of Christianity?

Did you feel a security and harmony in your home as a child?

Was your family structured according to the Ephesians model? (Ephesians 5:22-6:2)

How did your mother and father treat each other and you?

Were your parents overly strict, overly permissive, or _____? Explain.

Were either involved in adulterous affairs?

Is there a history of addictions? Name the addictions.

Name any occult, cultic, or non-Christian practices your parents or other ancestors may have been involved in.

Do you have any addictions or cravings that are hard to control? List.

Do you sleep well at night? If not, why not? (Ex: nightmares)

Are you adopted?

Have you ever been physically beaten or molested?

Do you hear voices?

Are you on any medications? List.

Section 6: Ministry Helps

Is prayer difficult for you?

Are you presently struggling with:

___daydreaming

___lustful thoughts

___inferiority

___worry/fear

___doubts

___fantasy

___obsessive/compulsive thoughts

___dizziness

___blasphemous thoughts

___bitterness/unforgiveness

___depression

___malice

___sudden bursts of anger

___dark, gloomy thoughts

_____

When at church, do you have negative thoughts against other Christians?
(Ex: wishing something bad would happen to someone in the service)

If you were to die tonight, where would you spend eternity?

Moving On

Personal Evaluation

Place a check next to any of these symptoms that you are experiencing:

☐ 1. You exaggerate, brag, or name-drop.

☐ 2. You are afraid to try new things for fear you will fail.

☐ 3. You adapt your opinions to others so they will like you.

☐ 4. You rely on addictive/compulsive behavior to numb your emotional pain.

☐ 5. You have a hard time making yourself be around people because you feel intimidated.

☐ 6. Your private self is different from your public self.

☐ 7. You frequently feel depressed.

☐ 8. You blame yourself when someone hurts you.

☐ 9. You frequently make excuses for those who mistreat you.

☐ 10. You act differently than you really are.

☐ 11. You try to solve the problems of others while neglecting your own life.

☐ 12. You are critical, focusing on the failures of others.

☐ 13. You like to dress, act, or behave in ways that are socially unacceptable.

☐ 14. You mostly spend time with people on an extreme end of the social ladder.

☐ 15. You back away from relationships with people you admire before they get to know you.

Section 6: Ministry Helps

☐ 16. You make unreal demands on yourself.

☐ 17. You feel lonely.

☐ 18. You are a perfectionist.

☐ 19. You feel people would not like you if they knew the real you.

☐ 20. You sometimes feel suicidal.

☐ 21. It is hard to ask for help because you feel admitting your need shows everyone your inadequacy.

☐ 22. You resist setting personal goals.

Choose 3 or 4 of the most prevalent characteristics you checked and give a recent example for each. God heals what we expose to Him. (1 John 1:9)

Section 6: Ministry Helps

Dear Wife,

Recently _____ has taken a very important step by joining the *Victory's Journey Moving On* support group. He probably did so with fear and mixed emotions, yet recognizing a need for healing in some areas concerning his past. He may be feeling unsure if he really wants to look at the problem, let alone have others "looking". It is a difficult place to be and that is where your role becomes extremely important.

As the support group continues through these next several months he may need some time to work these thoughts out. He is going to be digging up memories and pain that he has been avoiding for possibly a long time. This process is necessary in order for healing to follow. He will be dealing with, and working through, pains of the past and feelings of guilt and anger, as well as learning to receive God's forgiveness and to forgive others. He may need to work through the grieving process. This process of working through the pain may cause him to feel vulnerable.

What is your role in this process? How can you be a help? In your own way, give him all the support you can. Encourage him to take the time necessary to work through his pain. Also encourage him to come to each meeting. There will be all sorts of temptations and excuses not to attend meetings. Sometimes he will want to talk and sometimes he will not. We trust that you will love, support, protect, and help him in any way you can.

We are obligated to maintain confidentiality, but if we can help you to help your spouse or if you need assistance or have questions, please do not hesitate to call us. Thank you so much.

Cordially,

The VJ Leadership

Moving On

Dear Friend,

Recently_____ has taken a very important step by joining the *Victory's Journey Moving On* support group. This was probably done with fear and mixed emotions, yet with recognition of a need for healing in some areas concerning the past. Your friend may be feeling unsure if he/she really wants to look at the problem, let alone have others "looking". It is a difficult place to be and that is where your role becomes extremely important.

As the support group continues through these next several months your friend may need some time to work these thoughts out. He/she is going to be digging up memories and pain that he/she has been avoiding for possibly a long time. This process is necessary in order for healing to follow. There will be things to be dealt with and worked through, there will be revisited pain and feelings of guilt and anger. Most importantly, there will be a time of learning to receive God's forgiveness and to give forgiveness to others. He/she may need to work through the grieving process. This process of working through the pain may cause feelings of vulnerability.

What is your role in this process? How can you be a help? In your own way, give him/her all the support you can. Encourage your friend to take the time necessary to work through this pain. Also encourage him/her to come to each meeting. There will be all sorts of temptations and excuses not to attend meetings. Sometimes he/she will want to talk and sometimes not. We trust that you will love, support, protect, and help in any way you can.

We are obligated to maintain confidentiality, but if we can help you to help your friend or if you need assistance or have questions, please do not hesitate to call us. Thank you so much.

Cordially,

The VJ Leadership

Rev. Laverne Weber

1633 Mine Lane Rd.

Easton, PA 18045

Permission is given to copy forms, letters and handouts in this Victory's Journey manual for ministry purposes only. No other portion of this book may be reproduced, stored in a retrieval system, or transmitted in any form or by any means -electronic, mechanical, photocopy, recording, or any other - without the prior permission of one of the authors.

Our prayer is that God would bless you in your ministry of hope and healing to the hurting members of Christ's Body.

In Him,

Laverne Weber

Heidi Gregory

pastorlaverne@faithcom-ag.org

Victory's Journey Ministries

This is to certify that _____ *has completed the*

Victory's Journey Moving On program on _____, _____.

You are to be commended for your hard work and perseverance. May the Lord carry on to completion the work He has begun in your life!

_____   _____
Leader, Victory's Journey Ministries   Leader, Victory's Journey Ministries

ABOUT THE AUTHOR

Laverne Weber is an ordained minister with a specific calling and God-given ability to reach those who are hurting. She is also a nurse, teacher, and speaker who delivers life-changing truth filled with compassion and humor. She received her calling into the Lord's service as a missionary child in Sierra Leone, West Africa.

In 1993, Laverne founded *Victory's Journey*™ *Ministries*, formerly Journey to Joy, a ministry for those who are broken. She also serves with her husband as part-time pastors at Faith Community Assembly of God in Easton. The Webers have three children and four grandchildren.

It is one of her greatest joys to see the Holy Spirit set God's children free to grow into His purpose for them.

www.ingramcontent.com/pod-product-compliance
Lightning Source LLC
Chambersburg PA
CBHW080413170426
43194CB00015B/2798